THE LORD OF THE RING

PHIL ANDERSON

Regal

From Gospel Light
Ventura, California, U.S.A.

PUBLISHED BY REGAL BOOKS
FROM GOSPEL LIGHT
VENTURA, CALIFORNIA, U.S.A.
PRINTED IN THE U.S.A.

Regal Books is a ministry of Gospel Light, a Christian publisher dedicated to serving the local church. We believe God's vision for Gospel Light is to provide church leaders with biblical, user-friendly materials that will help them evangelize, disciple and minister to children, youth and families.

It is our prayer that this Regal book will help you discover biblical truth for your own life and help you meet the needs of others. May God richly bless you.

For a free catalog of resources from Regal Books/Gospel Light, please call your Christian supplier or contact us at 1-800-4-GOSPEL *or* www.regalbooks.com.

Library of Congress Cataloging-in-Publication Data
Anderson, Phil.
  The lord of the ring / Phil Anderson.
    p. cm.
  Includes bibliographical references.
  ISBN 0-8307-4327-8 (t)
  1. Zinzendorf, Nicolaus Ludwig, Graf von, 1700-1760. 2. Moravians—Germany—Biography. I. Title.
  BX8593.Z6A68 2007
  284'.6092—dc22
  [B]   2006034786

1   2   3   4   5   6   7   8   9   10   /   10   09   08   07

Rights for publishing this book in other languages are contracted by Gospel Light Worldwide, the international nonprofit ministry of Gospel Light. Gospel Light Worldwide also provides publishing and technical assistance to international publishers dedicated to producing Sunday School and Vacation Bible School curricula and books in the languages of the world. For additional information, visit www.gospellightworldwide.org; write to Gospel Light Worldwide, P.O. Box 3875, Ventura, CA 93006; or send an e-mail to info@gospellightworldwide.org.

Contents

ACKNOWLEDGMENTS

This book has emerged from a remarkable international community known as 24-7 Prayer. The individuals who have been an encouragement, challenge and inspiration to me in retelling Zinzendorf's story are too numerous to mention individually, but I am grateful to you all.

My specific thanks are due to Lisa, Holly and Bethany Anderson, for sharing our home with a 300-year-old German for the past two years. Thanks also go toPete Greig for provoking me to write and for the hours he spent helping to shape the results into something readable. To Justin Blake and Markus Laegel for being co-pilgrims on the journey. To Pete Ward and Tim Harrold for shaping the community that sent us on our way. To the Moravian archivists in Herrnhut (Rudiger Kruger) and London (Lorraine Parsons) for their generosity in sharing their knowledge and resources. And to the Moravian historians both past and present upon whose work and scholarship I have leaned so heavily.

FOREWORD

How do you describe a character like Count Zinzendorf—a man of whom so much is spoken and so little known?

Statesman? Prayer warrior? Bold missionary strategist? Peacemaker? Poet? Zealot? Autocrat? Entrepreneur? Eighteenth-century enigma? Occasional heretic? A very human saint? A swashbuckling, globetrotting hero of the faith? Yes! All of the above and more. For—as Phil Anderson's exceptional new biography reveals—the startling life of this lesser-known German aristocrat was colorful, imperfect and profoundly important.

The Lord of the Ring reveals that Zinzendorf may rightfully be described as the godfather to many of our contemporary Christian movements. For example, the great missions thrust of the last 200 years can be traced back to him; and, as if that were not enough, he is also an inspirational figure for the current global prayer movement. Zinzendorf's lifelong priority of Christian unity has also lent impetus to the ecumenical agenda of the postwar years. On top of all this, Zinzendorf is a key figure in the history of the Moravian, the Methodist and the Salvation Army denominations. Here, then, is a man whose life casts a long shadow over millions of people, even upon those who know little about him.

Long before Friends of the Earth coined the phrase as their slogan, Zinzendorf was a man who "thought global and acted local." Best known for instigating the Moravian "hundred-year prayer meeting" in the German village of Hernnhut, he also mobilized the first great missionary push of the Reformation. From the quiet village of Hernnhut to the ends of the earth, Zinzendorf successfully propelled the life-changing gospel of salvation by faith in Jesus at a time when few people gave any thought to the plight of those beyond the bounds of Christendom.

Moravian mission continues to bear fruit around the world today. Right now, for instance, I'm in South Africa, where I am serving as a representative of the 24-7 prayer movement—a night-and-day prayer watch inspired by Zinzendorf that has spread all over the world in five years. Last week, I had the privilege of facilitating intercession in the British Houses of Parliament. This week, I have heard stories of Africans who are too poor to afford a prayer room, and gather instead around appointed rocks to cry out to Jesus. Earlier today, I happened to drive past a Moravian church—a testimony to that great missionary explosion ignited in Herrnhut more than 200 years ago. Phil Anderson's book gives a thrilling depiction of the way this mission took root near Cape Town, South Africa (and I won't spoil the story by rehearsing it here!).

I was particularly interested to learn that in Hernnhut, Zinzendorf fostered an enterprising approach to community. At a time when many in our generation are looking for radical models of community, whereby work, rest and prayer might intersect more meaningfully and sustainably, I'm sure this little-known aspect of Zinzendorf's legacy will fascinate other readers too.

Zinzendorf's remarkable life found its defining moment in a mysterious Rule of Life, centered on a vow he made with his friends as a university student and marked by a ring. Jesus Himself, of course, was the Lord of that ring. Phil Anderson captures this dimension of Zinzendorf's life to show a generation like ours Zinzendorf's model of authentic values—rules of life—by which to navigate the complexity of postmodernity.

At a time when Zinzendorf's life has so much to teach us, this book (apparently, and amazingly, the first serious biography in the English language in at least 50 years) is thrillingly pertinent. I have personally learned a great deal about one of my heroes, thanks to this timely book. I particularly appreciate the rigorous research and the integrity of the storytelling.

Phil has told a warts-and-all story. He does not place Zinzendorf on a heroic pedestal but admits to his various failings and foibles. He does it in such a way that Zinzendorf becomes more remarkable, not less, as his many achievements are thrown into relief against the evidence of his humanity.

The Lord of the Ring reveals not just how much we owe to Zinzendorf as a historical figure, but also how much we can learn from him about our present reality and even, perhaps, about our future. As such, this book is more than just a historical biography; it is also, I believe, a work of prophetic importance and insight for anyone today with a passion for prayer, a call to the nations, a burden for Christian unity or a desire to explore radical community.

Phil Anderson lives for all these values day to day. I've flown with him, eaten curry with him, and talked and prayed with him. Our kids have played together. Phil is the real deal. He's also one of the cleverest and most focused people I know, but he never shows off about it. He is sacrificial, gentle, humble and fun—eminently qualified to write this book.

The writer of the book of Hebrews lists many great heroes of the faith and calls us to run the race with perseverance, our eyes fixed on Jesus, drawing inspiration from the "cloud of witnesses" cheering us on. One such witness, urging us on as we give ourselves to prayer, mission, unity and community is surely Count Zinzendorf, whose star is rising happily in our time. May his example galvanize us afresh to focus our ambitions entirely upon the Lord Jesus Christ.

Pete Greig
(www.24-7prayer.com)
Johannesburg, South Africa

Introduction

There is properly no history, only biography.

RALPH WALDO EMERSON

At the beginning of the twenty-first century, it seems that Christians everywhere are suddenly talking about Count Zinzendorf. As the Church in the postmodern, post-Christian West struggles to come to terms with her calling and mission in a new millennium, Zinzendorf and the eighteenth-century Moravian renewal, which he led, are increasingly viewed as an inspirational model.

Zinzendorf's impact on history has been profound. His legacy has shaped the lives of people groups from the British to the Mohican Indians, the Afro-Caribbeans and the Greenland Eskimos. His influence has touched personalities as diverse as William Carey, Dietrich Bonhoeffer and Nelson Mandela. If you want to understand why the West Indies are known for their vibrant gospel music or why the First Great Awakening swept across England and America through the Spirit-empowered preaching of John Wesley and George Whitfield, trace the answers and they will eventually lead you to Zinzendorf.

Intercessors look to the Moravian "100-year prayer watch" as the benchmark for serious prayer warriors. Evangelicals identify the Moravians as key initiators of revival and the architects of modern missions. Charismatics see the Pentecostal visitation of 1727 as a defining example of the Holy Spirit's transforming work. Advocates of church unity acknowledge that Zinzendorf coined the very word that defines their hopes ("ecumenism"). Postmodern emergents encounter the sense of identity and deeper

spirituality their culture longs to embrace in Zinzendorf's enig-
matic Order of the Mustard Seed. Contemporary Moravians and
Lutherans seek to rediscover their heritage, and Methodists are
recognizing that there may be more to their Moravian roots than
the hit-and-run "conversion" of their founder John Wesley.

For someone who has impacted our lives in so many ways,
most people are surprisingly ignorant of Zinzendorf. When he
is cited at all, it is normally in support of those groups who have
transiently adopted him as their "patron saint." It is as if history has kidnapped Zinzendorf, and all that we are allowed to see
is an occasional glimpse or a momentarily relevant facet of his
life and work.

I initially came to know about Zinzendorf through exactly
this route. Until a few years ago, my knowledge of the Moravians
was limited to vague recollections from a Methodist upbringing
of a mysterious group that emerged from nowhere, dramatically influenced the life of John Wesley, then vanished as quickly as
they had appeared. Then, in 2001, I encountered a remarkable,
accidental, international prayer movement known as 24-7 Prayer.
This movement had a crazy vision for young people to pray
day and night, around the clock. What was even crazier was
that it seemed to work. Their inspiration had been a seemingly chance visit by founder Pete Greig to Herrnhut in Germany,
the place where Zinzendorf had initiated the Moravian prayer
watch that ran without ceasing for 100 years.[1] So this was
Zinzendorf (or so I thought), the Great Prayer Leader. Patron
Saint of 24-7. One of Us.

At the end of 2003, Pete was starting work on a book inspired
by Zinzendorf's remarkable Rule of Life.[2] My task during the
occasional spare evening was to clarify the facts surrounding
Zinzendorf's semi-secret childhood spiritual society, the Order of
the Mustard Seed. A few months into this process, we had tracked
down enough material for the book, and 10 times more besides.

It was finally getting through to us that there was a lot more to the eighteenth-century Moravians than prayer, spiritual orders, overseas missions, or any of the many other filters through which they had previously been viewed. In Zinzendorf and his followers, we were forced to acknowledge that we could see the original DNA of our entire movement, as well as some crucial signposts for anyone who is grappling with the Church's authentic, relational and missional identity in a new millennium.

With several historical accounts to draw on but no contemporary version currently in print, it was Pete (again) who suggested that we needed to write a book specifically devoted to Zinzendorf. I was up for the challenge, but my personal style leans more toward Indiana Jones than the Library of Congress. I needed to see the places for myself, to touch, feel and smell as well as simply to read. I needed to understand Zinzendorf through the experience of pilgrimage alongside the discipline of research.

This book is the product of that journey. A journey that spans half of a continent and 300 years of history. A story through which I hope we will allow Zinzendorf to shape us with his vision, rather than seek to shape him through our interpretation. A quest whose ultimate goal and destination is Jesus Christ, to whom Zinzendorf gave his life in service.

Please fasten your seatbelts . . .

CHAPTER I

LITTLE LUTZ

Christianity began as a youth mission.
ARCHBISHOP GEORGE CAREY

The count was not an old man, but as he lay in an upper room of his Dresden home, he knew that he was going to die. Under the rich silk bedclothes, his body was emaciated, ribs protruding starkly from a collapsed chest, his neck unnaturally elongated behind knotted sinews. The racking coughs of consumption (tuberculosis) were growing weaker as his body gradually lost the capacity to fight the illness.

Gathering his remaining strength, Count George Ludwig von Zinzendorf reached for a small bell and rang for the servant who waited attentively outside the door of his chamber. Motioning the young man to draw closer, the count raised himself up and drew breath as if to speak, but instead lapsed into another coughing fit, showering the servant's face with droplets of spittle. Finally, in a faltering voice that still carried an unmistakable air of command, the count asked that his six-week-old son be brought to his bedside.

The footman's steps retreated down the staircase, to be replaced in a few moments by the lighter nervous tread of the nursemaid. She entered cautiously, the baby well wrapped in spite of the early summer warmth. Young Nikolaus Ludwig remained fast asleep, his face peaceful, a few wisps of golden hair offering a hint of the future head of blond curls that his father would never see. Taking the infant in his arms, George Ludwig slowly pronounced a final blessing over his child: "My dear son, they ask me to bless you, but you are more blessed than I am; even though now I feel as if I were already standing before the throne of Jesus."[1]

George Ludwig von Zinzendorf died on the nineteenth of July 1700, at the age of 38. He left behind his 25-year-old widow, Charlotte Justine; her firstborn son, Nikolaus Ludwig; and two children by his previous marriage.

Keeping It in the Family

To be widowed at such a young age left the countess in a delicate situation. There was money in the family, but none of it was immediately due to her, which left her dependent on the generosity of relatives for support. Hers had been no marriage of convenience; the couple had been close both emotionally and spiritually, and Charlotte's grief and loneliness were painful. For three years she lived with her infant son on her mother's estate at Gross Hennersdorf. In 1704, she remarried, becoming the wife of Field Marshal Dubislaw von Natzmer, a widower 20 years her senior who lived in Berlin.

It was then agreed that four-year-old Nikolaus Ludwig should remain in the care of his grandmother Henrietta. The formidable Lady von Gersdorf would now become the central figure in his upbringing. She affectionately nicknamed him Lutz, a name that stayed with him throughout his early childhood.

Right from the start, matters of faith took prominence in young Lutz's life. Both of his parents had shared deep Christian convictions, and his grandmother's estate at Gross Hennersdorf was an important meeting place for the movement of which they had been a part. Lutz lived in a household where spirituality was central to daily life rather than a mere Sunday ritual—

a home environment quite different from that of the majority of his contemporaries.

A Child of His Times

The eighteenth century was a time of great social change. In England, the Industrial Revolution was beginning, and with it a profound transition from rural lifestyles, which had not changed for centuries, to increased urbanization. In America, the Caribbean, Africa, India and the Far East, the European colonial powers were steadily extending their dominance. The age of global empires had begun. Across the world, the new social and political philosophies of the Enlightenment were emerging, which, by the end of the century, would sweep away the last remains of medieval feudalism in the American and French revolutions.

While society around it was undergoing dynamic changes, the Church on the whole had become divided and politicized. It bore little resemblance to the kind of discipleship that Jesus demanded and that His early followers lived out. Churches were strongly associated with the state, and unofficial sects were branded as theologically heretical and politically treasonous. In the previous century, Europe had been torn apart by a series of wars fought under religious banners between the mainly Protestant states of the north and the traditionally Catholic powers of the south. Even now, the military and political aftershocks continued, and psychological scars ran deep. Identifying oneself as Protestant, Catholic, Lutheran or Anglican became more often a statement of social and political allegiance than personal conviction.

The tradition in which the young Count Zinzendorf was brought up was a grass-roots renewal movement known as Pietism. First advanced by Philip Spener (himself a regular

visitor to Gross Hennersdorf), it emphasized the necessity of a
living relationship with Christ as Savior rather than external
religious affiliation. To our modern ears, the term "piety" in-
vokes images of a dreary, legalistic mind-set. In its later forms it
could indeed become narrow and dogmatic. To refer to someone as "pious" today is more likely to be taken as a criticism
than a compliment. But little Lutz was growing up during the
movement's vibrant and creative beginnings, when Pietism was
a generally healthy reaction against the nominalism of the
established churches.

Pietists formed religious societies that met together for
prayer, Bible study and discussion. In many ways they were the
first modern expression of the house church or cell concept.
Most Pietists, however, remained loyal to the state-sponsored
Lutheran Church, while also pursuing their unofficial spiritual
activities. Luther reflected in his Smalcald articles that meeting
together for fellowship was indeed a legitimate expression of
Christian faith and a means of God's grace. As a result, tensions
between traditional Lutherans and Pietists took shape as a
theological fence fight and rarely escalated into open conflict.

As every parent knows, there is no guarantee that the values
and beliefs of the family will be reproduced in the children, no
matter how sincerely those beliefs are held. In the Zinzendorf
family's case, however, Lutz immediately began to display a
deep childlike faith that amazed even his devout relatives. "In
my fourth year," he later wrote, "I began to seek God earnestly,
and determined to become a true servant of Jesus Christ."[2] At
the age of six, he was sometimes found talking to himself, and
would cheerfully confirm that he was speaking to Jesus, whom
he regarded as a kind of elder brother. As he learned to write
under his private tutor Edeling, he penned letters to his Savior
and threw them out the window in full confidence that Christ
would find and read them.

Growing up without a father and with only occasional contact with his mother, Zinzendorf's was a rather solitary childhood. Gross Hennersdorf was very much an adult world, and although playmates were arranged, they did not seem to feature largely in young Lutz's life. It was his aunt, a young woman in her early twenties also named Henrietta, who became his friend and confidante, part mother and part older sister. She prayed with Lutz daily, and his own prayer life soon progressed far beyond repeating the formal prayers he heard at church. "A thousand times," he said, "I heard Him speak in my heart, and saw Him with the eye of faith."[3] Only once, at the age of eight, does he record being troubled by atheistic doubts, and even these seem soon to have passed after a sleepless night of wrestling.

Young Nick's School Days

The plan for Zinzendorf's education may sound familiar: go to school, continue on to university, take a year out to travel and see the world, then get a job in the family business. But what is normal for thousands of young men and women in Western societies today was only feasible for a privileged minority in the early 1700s. At the age of 10, the young count was sent to attend the renowned Pietist boarding school at Halle near Leipzig.

On arrival, he accidentally overheard his mother in private conversation with the headmaster, August Hermann Francke. She described her son as a boy of great ability but needing to be kept in check or he would become proud and presume upon his talents.[4] The Pietism of Halle was already drifting toward a rigid view that regarded the human spirit as completely corrupt before the moment of conversion and fully redeemed thereafter. This model could not accommodate the spontaneous and joyful faith of the young Zinzendorf, so Francke initially wrote him off as unrepentant and deluded. This set the scene for the most miserable few years of Zinzendorf's life.

The tutors at Halle took his mother's warning and their own assumptions to heart and set out to break Zinzendorf of his pride. He was given menial tasks and was beaten for the most trivial of offences. The punishments were made into a form of public entertainment: "Next week," ran one announcement on the school notice board, "the count is to have the stick."[5] To avoid any sense of academic excellence, he was placed in classes below his ability; and when he became unmotivated, he was accused of laziness. On one occasion, imitation donkey ears were placed upon his head, and he was forced to stand at the front of the class with a sign that read "lazy donkey" on his back.

If the tutors were harsh with the young count, his fellow pupils were cruel in the way that only children can be. The sheltered environment of his youth, growing up surrounded by women and having inherited his father's relatively weak constitution, failed to equip him for the tough and ruthless environment of boarding school life. His noble origins only added to the problem. He easily outranked his peers in wealth and status, and they took every opportunity to bring him down a peg or two. Among the many taunts and practical jokes, his peers frequently knocked his books into the gutter, and then zealously reported him late for school while he picked up the mess. "With a few exceptions," he says sadly, "my schoolfellows hated me throughout."

His personal tutor, Daniel Crisenius, was the final straw. Appointed in 1712, Crisenius was a bully who made Zinzendorf's life a misery. Zinzendorf's grandmother opposed the appointment because she had doubts about Crisenius's character and felt that his piety was at best skin deep. Zinzendorf's Uncle Otto, however, considered Crisenius to be a shrewd man of the world. Between the two, his grandmother and uncle seemed to have had Crisenius pretty well worked out. He made Zinzendorf beg his relatives for money and then took most of it for himself. He advised the boy to write home complaining about his harsh treatment, then confiscated the letters and showed them to the school inspector. Crisenius did his best to interrupt the boy's prayers and devotions, and introduced crude topics of conversation to embarrass his pupil.

In spite of the tough conditions, Zinzendorf gradually began to shine academically. He was competent in Greek, fluent in French and Latin, and while he struggled with Hebrew, he excelled at poetry and public speaking. He was confirmed as a member of the Lutheran Church, and following his first communion wrote a moving hymn expressing his deep feelings at the event. Professor Francke began to reevaluate the young man more favorably and although he would never have admitted it, even Crisenius must have been cautiously impressed. By his final year, Zinzendorf had effectively completed the Halle curriculum and was placed in a small group of advanced students to prepare for his move up to university.

The Counter-Revolution

Although his academic progress must have given him some comfort, the most important aspect of Zinzendorf's final years at Halle was his spiritual involvement. His isolation did not last forever, and the friends to whom he was eventually drawn were those who shared his deep faith and convictions. They included George von Söhlenthal (the initial ringleader of the group), Anton von Wallbaum and Frederick de Watteville, who would remain one of his closest lifelong friends.

This group of friends, and numbers of others, began to meet in their rooms and in secluded spots around the school for prayer, Bible study, discussion and fellowship. Some of their schoolmates openly rebelled against their Pietist upbringing and education, but others wanted to emulate the example of a church within the church that they had seen. Zinzendorf proved himself to be a natural leader and organizer of these gatherings. He had an easy manner and was willing to talk to almost anyone on spiritual topics. The transformation was remarkable. He had progressed from being a lonely, bullied outsider into a role as one of the key movers in what amounted to a miniature spiritual revival. By the time he left Halle, he was able to hand over to Professor Francke details of no less than seven prayer groups and societies with which he had been involved. The staff subsequently went on to use these groups as the basis for a renewal of spiritual life amongst the students.[6]

One of the "privileges" of Zinzendorf's noble rank was that he got to have dinner every day at Francke's personal table. Initially this had been a painful experience, rubbing salt in the wounds of their strained relationship. However, in his final two years, a genuine friendship developed, and in addition to enjoying the older man's conversation, Zinzendorf had a chance to meet with many intriguing guests. In the early eighteenth century, Halle was one of the very few places in the Protestant world to have any developed concept of Christian mission. The idea that anyone should go and take the gospel message to people who had not yet heard it was simply alien to most branches of the Church. Halle, on the other hand, had already sent out a handful of foreign missionaries under the patronage of the Danish royal family.

One of these very first missionaries was Ziegenbalg, who had gone to the Indian colony of Tranquebar. Zinzendorf met him while he was back on furlough in 1715 and was deeply impressed by his stories of serving Christ overseas. De Watteville shared his friend's enthusiasm, and the two of them entered into a solemn agreement to promote the missionary cause in their futures. Neither De Watteville nor Zinzendorf expected to be able to go in person, but they resolved to send whoever God might show them to the people overseas about whose spiritual welfare no one else seemed to care.

For the five friends at the center of the new move of faith at Halle, occasional meetings for prayer and fellowship would never be enough. They fully intended to commit their lives to the service of Christ and started to look for ways to express that commitment in practice. In purely natural terms, their wealth and rank would give them ample opportunities for self-indulgence. Their expression of teenage rebellion would be to live in a way that was holy in every respect and worthy of being called true disciples of Jesus. In 1715, they formed a new society, committing together to live lives of righteousness before God and genuine accountability before each other. They called their group the "Slaves of Virtue" and met together in a spirit of frank honesty and mutual encouragement.

In early 1716, Zinzendorf went home to spend a few months on his grandmother's estate prior to starting at university. He had gone to Halle as a precocious but slightly spoiled child. He returned older, wiser, and having learned some of life's lessons the hard way. He had also made some enduring friendships that would last for the rest of his life. Although none of them yet knew it, their society of five was destined to become a covenant community that would eventually include among its members people of influence throughout the whole of the known world.

Southend Airport, East of London, UK
Wednesday, June 02, 2004, 09:20 GMT

"Clear Prop!"

I shout the statutory warning out of the small Perspex window next to the pilot's seat and hit the starter. The propeller cranks over with a reluctant whine, then the first cylinder fires and the engine growls into life. Quickly I run through the post-start checks. Oil pressure, fuel pressure, temperature, amps, suction. I glance over at Justin Blake, who is sitting next to me in the right-hand seat. He looks relaxed but quietly excited. I don't blame him. In an age of sanitized mass transportation, there is something about flying in a small airplane that stirs a sense of genuine adventure.

We give the engine a few minutes to warm up and turn on the radio and satellite navigation systems. Our course, carefully marked out on five separate charts, threads its way through the congested airspace of Western Europe and on to Dresden in the east of Germany. We have already filed a flight plan for Antwerp in Belgium, the first of two planned stops en route.

Together we plan to traverse 600 miles and three centuries, to another land and another time. The ultimate destination of our journey is the village of Herrnhut, tucked away in the farthest corner of Germany near the Polish and Czech borders. Nearly 300 years ago, this obscure setting was the scene of a remarkable spiritual revival. Under the leadership of a charismatic nobleman named Nikolaus Ludwig von Zinzendorf, an unlikely community became for a time the world's most dynamic powerhouse of Christian mission and renewal.

The reason we are setting out on this crazy journey—part adventure, part research trip, part pilgrimage—is much more recent. One of the lasting achievements of the Herrnhutters was the establishment of a continuous prayer watch, which ran day and night for 100 years. In 1999, inspired and challenged by the example of the Herrnhut "Moravians,"[7] a group of young people in Chichester on the south coast of England decided to see if they could manage to do the same thing for a month. The result was the unexpected birth of a movement known as 24-7 Prayer. In five years, with no grand strategy, no big-name leadership and almost no budget, the wave of continuous prayer has spread to over 50 countries and seen thousands of mainly young people praying and encountering God like never before.[8] Justin was part of 24-7 from the beginning. I came to it slightly later, drawn in initially by a friend called Tim Harrold, who had there found the fulfillment of his own dreams of seeing youth turn to God in prayer. Now we are going to the place where it all began, to try to better understand the spiritual heritage of the movement in which we are both caught up.

The oil temperature needle is moving at last, and it's time to go. I select the radio frequency and press the transmit button: "Southend Tower, Golf Foxtrot Mike Alpha Mike."

The call-sign (normally abbreviated to "Alpha Mike") is our means of identification and the nearest our airplane has to a name. Technically, the aircraft is a *Piper PA-28 Warrior,* owned by a six-person syndicate based at Southend. Emotionally, it is the culmination of a dream flight, which I have harbored since childhood. Every step along my aeronautical journey has brought a new challenge, and this ambitious flight across Europe is pushing the bar up another notch.

"Alpha Mike, taxi holding point Alpha runway Two-Four."

Alpha Mike trembles in the slipstream of 160 horsepower, and I reach down and release the brakes. A slight pressure on the rudder pedals to keep the nose straight, a glance down at the airspeed indicator, as we reach 64 knots, I pull smoothly back on the control column, and we are airborne. Leveling out at 2,000 feet, we cross the Thames Estuary and set course for Dover, the first leg of our journey.

Crossing open water in a single-engined aircraft always tends to focus the pilot's mind. As we approach the coast, I open the throttle and raise the nose, gaining as much extra height as conditions will allow. It won't save us from a swim if the engine were to give up half way, but it might at least earn us the time and gliding distance to find a friendly boat to ditch next to.

Our short hop over the narrowest stretch of the English Channel passes without incident. We skirt the exclusion zone around the French nuclear power station at Gravelines, and then request clearance to pass over the Belgian coastal airport of Ostend. So far so good, but according to the forecasts, the trickiest bit of the flight is yet to come.

Unlike commercial airliners cruising at over 30,000 feet, small airplanes are quite vulnerable to the changing weather. Low cloud, fog, thunderstorms or strong winds can all make conditions unsafe for us. For the last few days, the Internet weather services have been predicting that a band of low cloud and rain will be lying across our path somewhere over the Low Countries. Since the beginning of the week, we and a number of our friends have been praying that the system would weaken, or the whole trip would have to be cancelled. Even as late as breakfast this morning, we didn't make our decision until a final check revealed that the 12-hour forecasts for southern Holland looked flyable. As we track inland across Belgium, the moment of truth has arrived.

The broken cloud over the Channel has now been replaced by a leaden overcast. The cloud base lowers steadily, forcing us down below 1,000 feet. With only 15 miles to run to Antwerp, I call them up on the radio. By the time I select the new frequency and make contact, we have been pushed lower still and it starts to rain. Tension in the cockpit is rising; low flying is much more exacting, and navigation is becoming harder in the worsening visibility. I pass our flight details, but the answer from Antwerp confirms what I already know. "Alpha Mike, we cannot accept a visual flight. Please leave our zone and remain clear of controlled airspace."

Taking a quick look at the map, we see that there is a small airfield about 20 miles to the northwest on the Dutch coast that should have clearer weather. We announce our new destination as Midden-Zeeland. Antwerp transfers us to Dutch Military Radar, whose worried-sounding controller advises us to steer a course of 305 degrees magnetic. Planning and executing a diversion at low level in poor weather in the cramped cockpit of a light aircraft is not an easy task. In this case, however, I am on top of the situation, and 10 minutes later the airstrip at Midden-Zeeland comes into view.

As expected, the conditions here are better and we fly a conventional circuit to land. Touching down on the neat grass runway, it is good to be back on the ground, but our faces betray our concern. Unless we can find a way through this weather system, our journey could be over almost before it has begun.

CHAPTER 2

THE FELLOWSHIP
OF THE RING

I will take the ring, though I do not know the way.

FRODO

What do the Archbishop of Canterbury, the King of Denmark and an Indian chief have in common?" Sounds like it could be the opening line of a rather corny joke; however, in 1737, the very same question came close to causing an international scandal. It started routinely enough. A Prussian officer by the name of Abraham von Rumswinkel, stationed in Amsterdam, died, and there were found among his possessions a set of papers and a gold ring bearing an inscription in Greek. The papers proved that von Rumswinkel had been a member of some kind of secret society. These papers included a provision that they should not be made public and must be returned to the order's "secretary" following the death of a member. The "secretary" was none other than Count Nikolaus Ludwig von Zinzendorf, by then a controversial public figure.

The unfortunate Rumswinkel had clearly failed to organize his demise in the specified manner. The papers instead came into the hands of a Professor Voget of Utrecht, who was keen to use them to stir up trouble for Zinzendorf. He published extracts from them as part of a tract in 1738, and in his commentary used them to imply that the members of Zinzendorf's community were secretive political agitators.[1]

To set the record straight, Zinzendorf reluctantly arranged for the full text of the rules of the order to be published. This was done in Büdingen in 1740, and copies still survive today. They offer a remarkable insight into a covenant that Zinzendorf had first entered into as a teenager but which grew to include some of the leading figures of his day, including kings, bishops, governors and even the chief of the Creek Indian nation.

Finishing School

As the spring of 1716 drew to a close, Zinzendorf longed to return to Halle to study theology. After a difficult few years, his relationship with Professor Francke was at an all-time high, and he had formed close friendships with others who shared his zeal and spiritual ambitions. However, his Uncle Otto (who was acting as a legal guardian) had little sympathy for the Pietists at Halle. Saxony was a Lutheran kingdom and, according to Otto, the young count therefore needed a more orthodox conclusion to his education. Zinzendorf was bundled off to the Lutheran University of Wittenberg to follow in his father's footsteps and train for the legal profession.

On the academic side, Zinzendorf set about his legal studies with competence, if not exactly much personal enthusiasm. Even with his blue blood and charm, he wasn't able to gatecrash the theology lectures going on next door, but he did cultivate close relationships with some of the professors who gave them. He attended the Lutheran church diligently and listened to the sermons with an open but considered respect. He also read carefully the works of Luther and those of his Pietist occasional critic, Spener.

For an eighteenth-century nobleman, university was as much about cultivating social skills as learning those that were purely academic. The curriculum at the university involved riding, fencing, dancing and card playing. Extracurricular activities frequently included heavy drinking, dueling and getting a foot on the first rung of social and sexual politics. Zinzendorf was alarmed by the potential temptations and skeptical of the benefits these skills would bring. He prayed while he fenced—a tricky and potentially dangerous combination unless you are already expert in at least one of the two activities. He prayed, too, that he would quickly master the formal dance steps so as to avoid "wasting" his time on further lessons. He insisted that any money he won at cards would be given to charitable causes. He need not have worried too much on that front: His old tutor Daniel Crisenius had accompanied him as a kind of chaperon and took the opportunity to empty his pockets of a few more florins in the name of education in the university of life.

While settling into his new circumstances at Wittenberg, Zinzendorf kept up an enthusiastic correspondence with his old friends from Halle. Their final act of commitment to one another while still at school had been to form the accountability group they called the "Slaves of Virtue." Now, with the opportunities and temptations of university life opening up before them, they felt the need for a more formal and binding commitment to Christ and to each other.

Hard Days' Knight

The idea that began to take shape in Zinzendorf's fertile and romantic imagination was that of a spiritual order of knighthood. He and his friends from university agreed to bind themselves to serve Christ their King faithfully in every life situation. The concept of a secret spiritual order sounds strange to our twenty-first-century minds,[2] but to these young men (most of whom owed their status and position to social structures and

traditions dating back to the Middle Ages), it seemed a perfect-
ly reasonable idea. They took a vow to support one another in
standing by the principles upon which they had agreed, and
created various rules and symbols to remind them of their commitments to Christ and to each other.

The initial name for the order was the "Confessors of Christ."
The first rules appear in a handwritten document signed by
the five school friends and dated "Anno 1716," the year that
Zinzendorf left Halle.[3] For their emblem they designed a medal-
lion, and Zinzendorf's grandmother had it made up as a sixteenth
birthday present. On the front was an image of the wounded
Christ and the words *"Vulnera Christi."* On the back an angel and
"Nostra Medela" were enameled. Together the words of the inscription translate as "Christ's wounds, our healing"—a reference to
Isaiah 53. Later on in his spiritual journey, the wounds of Christ
would become a central feature of Zinzendorf's spirituality.
As the young men continued to mature spiritually, their commitment matured with them. The heart of the covenant never changed,
but its expression developed as they made the transition from
school to university to positions of responsibility in society. The
twentieth-century Moravian bishop Herbert Spaugh summarizes
the objectives to which members committed themselves:

1. To be kind to all men
2. To be true to Christ
3. To send the gospel to the world[4]

Some time later, they added the best known and most enduring symbol of their order: a gold ring decorated in enamel and
inscribed with the Greek words that translate "None of us lives
for himself."[5]

In light of a progressing sense of vow, covenant and spirituality, the name for the order needed modification. The "Slaves of

Virtue" expressed a worthy ideal, but sounded a bit pompous. The "Confessors of Christ" made a grand declaration, but lacked subtlety and depth. Their new inspiration came straight from the authority and insight of the Bible. Jesus told His followers that the kingdom of God would be like a mustard seed, starting invisibly small but growing to become a great tree (see Matt. 13:31-32; Mark 4:30-32; Luke 13:18-19). He also threw a challenge, saying that if they had faith "even as small as a mustard seed," they could tell a mountain to jump into the sea and it would obey them (see Matt. 17:20; Luke 17:6). The new title, the "Order of the Mustard Seed," painted the perfect picture of a small group working privately but expecting big results, and of young people determined to live by faith as they faced the challenges of life.

They created a new emblem for the Order of the Mustard Seed, which was also a medallion: a cross with a picture of a mustard tree and a Latin inscription meaning "that which was formerly nothing" (by implication, "has become a great tree").

True to Christ

In a world where a veneer of religious devotion was often essential to get along in politics and society, the Order of the Mustard Seed made a clear distinction between outward show and a heart of genuine commitment. One article bluntly requires the following:

> There are many Christians whose salvation is genuine, but equally there are many people who claim to be "Christians" but are not actually true servants of the Lord. To be a member of this Order, you must be a genuine servant and follower of Christ.[6]

The structure of the order cut right across the social hierarchy of its day. They affirmed that:

Kings and Queens may become members of the Order,
but they do not automatically become leaders of it and
membership cannot be passed on or inherited. If anyone tries to misuse their membership for fame or personal advancement, they can no longer be a member
and must resign.

The members had considered in detail how they would apply
their principles of following Christ to real-world issues they
might face. The early rules majored on the temptations most relevant to young noblemen, including drinking, gambling and
dancing (plus, presumably, the associated après-dance activities).
Later editions addressed issues of judgment, including the balance between honesty and discretion, boldness and discernment.

The Order of the Mustard Seed chooses to stay secret
and to work out of the public eye.
    We intend to work in a way that is honest and up-
right. Even when we do things carefully and shrewdly, we
will never be dishonest or underhand.
    We will not be over-hasty, but will think carefully
before we act.
    We will not, however, think too long before stepping
through doors that have been opened by God. In everything we will be brave and joyful, whilst taking care not
to close other doors through our actions.

They recognized that their ultimate aim was not to impress
their contemporaries or even to attain great goals, but to live
faithfully before God. The final rule states:

When we have achieved all of these good aims, we will
not ask for any glory or reward from them. We will live

to the end of our days in the grace that comes from the cross of Christ alone. We will die willingly, because after hard labor comes a great reward.

Kind to All Men

The concept of sacrificial love, the New Testament *agape,* embodies the highest and finest ideals of Christian faith. The first article of the document makes it clear that:

> Every one of us commits to love and serve the whole human race through whatever position he finds himself in.

However, in practice Christians can sometimes be guilty of speaking and acting in a way that appears cruel or harsh, while claiming to do so "in love." It was with good reason that Herbert Spaugh identified the more practical virtue of kindness as the one to which the Order of the Mustard Seed committed themselves. Again, they had thought through in detail the circumstances that might challenge them to display that kindness mentioned in 1 Corinthians 13:4.

> If any of us has a personal opponent who is also a servant of God, and their work is going well, a member of the Order will support what their opponent is doing. This way even the things that our enemies do for God will prosper, and great blessing will come from our actions.
>
> Against the trend, we do not seek to abolish the old and establish the new. Instead we aim to sanctify and bring out the best in old traditions.
>
> Where there are institutions which were originally of God but have now become dark and useless, and God starts to renew them through his mercy, we will support

them in returning to their former glory.

Where anyone has a good intention or has made a promising start, we will support them wholehearted-ly. This will be so even when their plans are not yet fully worked out, so that out of it our common Lord may be glorified.

The structure of their organization reflected the spirit of servanthood, which they had committed to display in their lives.

Every member of the Order is equal in status. When someone is acting as the "secretary," they are there to be a contact point and to handle correspondence but not to take authority.

Zinzendorf was a persuasive and charismatic leader, but there is no evidence that he used the order to pressure others to exert influence on his behalf. The "conspiracy" was always to serve Christ, never his own particular plans or ambitions.

Gospel to the World

Zinzendorf and his friends had a well-developed concept of mission, in an age when it was poorly understood and seldom attempted. They recognized that "conversion" meant bringing individuals to a place of genuine and personal faith in Jesus, not persuading people to change their allegiance to a different branch of Christianity, as was then commonly assumed. They started with an explicit declaration of both their unity and their diversity in Christ:

Because of the state of the churches it is not possible to completely bring people together. We are divided by borders and nationality, by our professions, and by church backgrounds and ancestry. We are, however, united by the fact of our salvation through Jesus Christ, the Son of God, born of Mary. This then is the aim of our work in the whole world: that we reach the hearts of all for the sake of the One who gave his life for our souls.

They then made a specific declaration of intent relating to their mission:

> We desire to join the souls of all people to their Creator, and to their Saviour Jesus as soon as they come to know about him.

Their understanding of what mission was *not* was as clear as their vision of what it was:

> No one should try and persuade a new convert to join their own church when that person was won to Christ by Christians of a different background, as long as the person is going on in obedience to the cross. This only applies to "genuine" conversions, not the strange practice whereby someone never had Christ taught or explained to them but was forcibly converted or baptised.

Finally, they were ground-breakingly inclusive in their understanding of who was called to spread the gospel and how it should be worked out in practice:

> Everyone should work to further the kingdom of God within the context of their own profession. If you are a teacher, then teach for the Lord, etc.

To the members of the Order of the Mustard Seed, every follower of Christ was a missionary, whether at home or in the farthest corners of the earth. Thus, Zinzendorf and de Watteville
were not only committed to sending others overseas, but they
were equally determined to spread the gospel in whatever
context they found themselves.

Walking the Talk

The declaration of intent that Zinzendorf and his friends
wrote in a spirit of unity, open-handedness and mission-
minded faith is remarkable. That it was written with such
maturity and wisdom by a group of teenagers in the early 1700s,
in an environment where religious and political strife were the
norm, is exceptional. The Church today could learn a lot from
this type of covenant and needs to be humble enough to recognize that it is not necessarily well-known and established leaders
who are capable of providing vision and initiative.

Talk is often said to be cheap. Talk that is refined over several years before being adopted in a final form is perhaps a bit
more costly. Talk that deliberately sets its conspirators on a collision course with the social order and the powers that be has
the potential to be costlier still. There is every indication that
the Mustard Seed "conspirators" understood and were willing
to accept the price they might have to pay. One document
shows that a member bound himself "rather to lose his life,
than to depart from the faith."[7] In the turbulent world of the
early eighteenth century, this was a very real possibility.[8]

Zinzendorf attempted to put these principles into practice
when he boldly attempted to get the Lutheran university of
Wittenberg and the Pietist institution at Halle to bury the hatch-
et and make peace. He had already concluded that orthodox
Lutheranism could make space for the strong personal faith of

the Pietists. Likewise, he was sure that the Pietists could lay aside their rather sectarian outlook without compromising their principles. He started discussions with his friends and contacts in both institutions, and for a while it appeared that this 18-year-old diplomat might be able to pull off the unthinkable. In the end it never happened. His family became alarmed that he was getting out of his depth and instructed him to back off. Whether he was frustrated or secretly relieved is not recorded.

Despite this setback, the Mustard Seed covenant shows that Zinzendorf maintained grand ideals. His conduct while at university offers plenty of evidence that he was willing to knuckle down and live out those ideals in the nitty-gritty of everyday life. He avoided the free-and-easy lifestyle that many young nobles considered to be their right. He read the Bible regularly and set aside every Sunday for fasting and prayer. He was known to have been involved regularly in all-night prayer sessions (possibly as the only way of escaping smart-aleck remarks from Crisenius about his excessive piety). His social life inevitably suffered as a result. His peer group thought of him as slightly odd. Admittedly, he was a bit proud about his piety, which probably didn't help matters. On the whole, though, his go-for-it approach to faith and discipline made him friends among those whose opinions he valued. As for the rest, he wasn't interested in earning their respect anyway.

Zinzendorf's eye was already on God's longer-term purposes for his life. The choice of the mustard seed as an emblem reflected a genuine understanding that the kingdom of God grows gradually, through an individual life, a movement or a nation. As he would later write:

> The "mustard seed" is the emblem of the Order and its guiding principle, taken from Mark chapter 4 verses 30 to 32. We will work simply and quietly. Even if we never

see wonders with our own eyes or hear of them with our ears, we are planting the kingdom of heaven into the nations and will look for the fruit which grows from it.[9]

In fact, the fruit would begin to emerge sooner than anyone could have expected.

Midden-Zeeland Airfield, Holland
Wednesday, June 2, 2004, 13:00 GMT

As we climb up to the control tower to pay our landing fee and inquire about fuel, another English voice crackles out over the radio. He seems to be in exactly the same predicament as us and has also selected Midden-Zeeland as his preferred diversion. After an aborted approach caused by disorientation at the unfamiliar aerodrome, the Cessna makes it down on the second attempt and joins Alpha Mike on the grass near the pumps.

Meanwhile, Justin and I have retreated to the restaurant where we order omelets and salad. The pilot of the Cessna turns out to be an English gentleman who soon joins us at the next table. By a bizarre coincidence he has come from Goodwood, just a few miles from Justin's hometown of Chichester. I listen bemused as, on an obscure Dutch airstrip that none of us even intended to be at, they debate the relative merits of Indian restaurants in the Chichester area. Further conversation is restricted by the fact that the other pilot has left his hearing aid in the cockpit, so we finish our meal and head off to check out the weather.

While Justin and I try to figure out a plan, the gentleman from Goodwood comes back up to the control tower and announces that he has found a guesthouse for the night. The radar image on the Internet screen in front of us suggests that we might be well advised to do the same. A band of cloud and rain nearly 50 miles wide is sitting, immobile, from the north of Holland right down through Belgium and into France. At its eastern edge near the German border, a vicious line of yellow zigzags marks a cluster of thundershowers where the two air masses, which have created this mess, are colliding.

Wishful thinking about weather conditions has killed more pilots than mechanical failure or navigational errors. However, we have been praying about this trip for weeks, and so many apparently closed doors have already opened up. We are willing to believe now for just one more. The radar picture shows that the frontal system is far from uniform. The storm cells lie to the north and south of our current position, but due east there is evidence of a gap, which might be passable. Together we agree to give it a go. We file a flight plan for Paderborn in Germany and joke with the man in the control tower that we may be seeing him again within an hour.

Fully fueled up once again, Alpha Mike roars enthusiastically down the grass strip and into the grey overcast sky. We level out just below the clouds with the altimeter reading an encouraging 1,000 feet. Navigationally the route couldn't be simpler. We follow the map, threading our way across a network of inland seas toward the mouth of the Rhine. We are well into the weather band now and still maintaining 800 feet, with good visibility and not even a shower. A succession of huge river barges drift past below us: This part of the world may be flat and featureless from ground level, but from the air it is spectacular.

The estuary turns into a pair of rivers. We choose the Maas to maintain our easterly track. Dutch Military Information clears us to cross their airbase at Voget. The next checkpoint is the German border and it's really starting to look as if we are going to make it.

Ahead the cloud base loses its smooth appearance and starts to hang low and ragged, the first sign of approaching rain. Slowly we are pushed down: 700 feet, 600 feet, 500 feet. This is our absolute limit. Any lower, and I will simply have to turn back. Light rain starts to splatter the windscreen, and visibility drops as we enter a shower.

This is the moment of truth. We know for sure that only a few miles ahead lie clear skies, but that's no use to us if we can't break through the edge of the front. I try to give Justin as honest and objective an appraisal of the situation as I can muster. We both pray that God will open one more door and allow us to pass through. A straw poll of the spiritual sense in the cockpit still has two votes to nil in favor of "press on." The conditions stay the same for several endless minutes, tantalizingly on the edge of legality, good judgment and faith. The visibility begins to pick up again—we must be reaching the far side.

Then, suddenly, we are through. The plains of Germany spread out in front of us. The cloud base rises faster than Alpha Mike can climb, and in a couple of minutes we are cruising comfortably at 2,000 feet.

I still have a lot to learn about prayer. We have been laying the issue of weather before God in prayer for days, so why did this one have to go right to the wire? Why did we fail at Antwerp before succeeding along the Maas? Why, instead of an aerial equivalent of Moses parting the Red Sea, did we have to crawl through a tiny tear in a huge curtain of gray? Was our decision to push on commendable faith and trust, or reckless presumption that happened to turn out well?

Part of the reason for taking the raw and sometimes unpredictable option of flying to Herrnhut ourselves was a desire to explore the concept of pilgrimage. Taking a scheduled airline would have been more reliable and probably cheaper, but it would have robbed us of the experience of *journeying*. Pilgrims through the ages have always understood that the journey has as much to teach us about ourselves and our relationship with God as reaching the destination. Without the one, our experience of the other is impoverished. Now, God willing, we will reach Herrnhut not as tourists, but as those who have been through trials and overcome along the way.

CHAPTER 3

THE RETURN OF
THE KNIGHT

Christianity is more than a one-to-one relationship
between the individual and God, important as that is.
The relationship also has to be with the outside world.

TONY BLAIR

Dates with destiny are usually blind. As Zinzendorf walked into the fine, if not exactly world-renowned, Düsseldorf art gallery on a late spring afternoon, he had no idea of the impact the visit was going to have on him. He viewed the pictures with polite interest, until he came to a portrait depicting Jesus Christ at the moment of his condemnation to death.

The figure is dressed in a rough robe, with a coarse noose of rope around his neck and wrist. The face is slightly bowed, and small trails of blood run down from the crown of thorns forced onto his head. The eyes are momentarily averted, the invitation to the viewer coming instead from the complex expression of peace and pain, compassion and exhaustion passing across Christ's face. The dark background reflects the cruelty of the deed that is about to be perpetrated, but around the head is a glow of hope that transcends the surroundings without ever becoming the superficial "halo" of medieval convention. The scene is titled *Ecce Homo* (after Pontius Pilate's words to the crowd: "Behold the man") and is a fairly common subject in renaissance art. Under the portrait, the artist has written an inscription in Latin: "This I have done for you, what will you do for me?"[1]

When Christians talk of God speaking to them, they often describe a moment when something they have read or heard simply jumps off the page and grabs them in a way that is compelling beyond any purely intellectual or emotional reaction. This was just such a moment for Zinzendorf. He stood transfixed in front of the picture and its caption for over an hour. He knew that the question was directed to him and that it demanded an uncompromisingly absolute answer. "This I have done for you, what will you do for me?" There in the Düsseldorf gallery, he silently made his response to Jesus Christ and determined that he would give the rest of his life to the service of God.

It was perhaps inevitable that a work of art would be used to release a sense of personal calling equal to any of the intellectual commitments Zinzendorf had previously made. In an age of word-based reason and a Protestant tradition that fought shy of any artistic outlet beyond word and music, Zinzendorf had always embraced creative expression. In addition to his emerging talents as a poet and lyricist, he had interests and genuine ability in architecture, design and visual arts. Now he sensed that in that haunting image, God had provided him with a personal encounter with Christ, which he could neither forget nor ignore.

One for All, All for One

The visit to Düsseldorf marked the start of Zinzendorf's *Wanderjahr*—the grand tour of Europe without which a young nobleman's education could not be regarded as complete. Holland was then one of the key colonial and trading nations in Europe, and Zinzendorf's first stop was to be the city of Utrecht.

A postgraduate course in international law would be supplemented by a chance to mingle with one of the most influential high societies in the known world. He continued his studies and, as was expected of him, built up contacts with the Dutch establishment and court. His own agenda was slightly different, and he continued quietly to recruit small numbers of influential members to the Order of the Mustard Seed. It was one of these contacts, the young Prussian officer Abraham von Rumswinkel, whose death 20 years later was to be instrumental in revealing details of the order to the outside world.

A whistle-stop tour of the other major Dutch cities was followed by a final stay in Paris. The French capital was notorious for the high-living excesses of its noble elite, and the prospect of staying there was quite alarming to Zinzendorf. The lavish but callous attitudes of these spoiled aristocrats would, just 70 years later, be one of the factors triggering the French Revolution. Finding himself in need of a friend, Zinzendorf was delighted to discover that Nicholas de Watteville, the brother of his school friend Frederick, was also staying in the city. Their interests did not always coincide, however, as de Watteville wrote:

> We soon became very good friends and visited each other daily. But as to the disposition of our hearts, we differed greatly, notwithstanding our friendship. He introduced me to cardinals and bishops, but I could not persuade him to go to a single opera.[2]

At court, Zinzendorf was received by the prince regent and his mother, the dowager duchess. His reputation had clearly gone ahead of him. She politely teased him for not yet visiting the opera (which he confirmed), and asked if there was any truth in the rumor that he knew the entire Bible by heart (to which he replied, "Ah, I only wish I did!").[3]

Zinzendorf's rank was capable of opening more than just the palace doors, some of the most intriguing being those of the Catholic archbishop's residence. At nearly 70 years of age, Cardinal Louis-Antoine de Noailles was an interesting character. He came from a wealthy background but had a track record of concern and personal generosity toward the poor. His main achievements had been practical and pastoral: He published documents promoting the good conduct of worship in the churches of France and established a mandatory requirement for new priests to spend time in training before taking up office. This last measure made it much more difficult (or at least uncomfortable) for social climbers with no interest in spiritual matters to use the church as a means of personal advancement.[4]

The old cardinal and the young count struck up a surprising but genuine friendship and conversed regularly. De Noailles at first tried to convert Zinzendorf to Catholicism but was eventually broad-minded enough to accept him for the clearly sincere young man that he was. Zinzendorf discovered that genuine followers of Christ were not restricted to the Protestant churches as he had previously been taught. In these encounters, Zinzendorf's view of the Church as a single body, transcending all sectarian divisions, grew and took shape. De Noailles agreed to accept membership of the Order of the Mustard Seed—something that could have been damaging if made public and which illustrates the nonsectarian character of the order.

Their friendship continued through letter writing for a number of years until the archbishop became entangled in one of the theological controversies of his day (Jansenism[5]), and under direct pressure from Rome was forced to retract some of his statements and accept the party line. Zinzendorf was deeply disappointed that the bishop had caved in and rather ungraciously ended their correspondence. Clearly, although they had found much to admire in each other, Zinzendorf's stubborn idealism and de Noailles's pragmatism did not always make for an easy relationship!

Falling in Love

With his "year out" drawing to an end, Zinzendorf set out to return to Saxony. On the way back he decided to stop off and pay a courtesy visit to his aunt, the Countess of Castell. The visit was supposed to be brief, but shortly after arriving, Zinzendorf fell ill with a fever and remained stuck in bed for several weeks. The surroundings were hardly uncomfortable: The countess was a concerned and generous hostess, his cousin Theodora mopped his fevered brow attentively, and he was soon on the road to recovery.

Before leaving he offered to assist the countess with putting some of the administrative affairs of her estates in order, which she accepted with a knowing smile. The affairs took slightly longer than expected, which gave the young count plenty of time to engage in drawing room conversation and to participate in the social life of the house. He also became involved in the religious services of the estate, which further prolonged his stay. Finally it became obvious to everyone that Zinzendorf's continued presence had an ulterior motive, and that motive was Theodora.

Unlike the numerous young women who had either presented themselves to or thrown themselves at the count during his travels, Theodora was an attractive and socially acceptable potential bride. Her attitude was slightly cool but not unresponsive; she presented Zinzendorf with her portrait, which in the social customs of the day was considered to be a green light, rather like being offered a photo for your wallet. The respective mothers discussed the matter, and both countesses gave their blessing to the match. It was not until Zinzendorf had a chance meeting

with his old friend Henry von Reuss that the full picture became apparent.

Reuss had affections for Theodora that went back farther
than Zinzendorf's, and his appearance on the scene had left both
of them secretly dismayed. As the senior in rank, protocol gave
Zinzendorf first refusal, but inside he was torn. He was thoroughly smitten with Theodora, but equally dismayed with the
prospect of trampling over the emotions of his lovesick friend.
The opportunity to reflect had also set some alarm bells ringing.
Sincere as Theodora was, she had so far shown little real empa-
thy for Zinzendorf's burning sense of spiritual calling.

Reuss and Zinzendorf journeyed back to Castell together,
and the true situation became increasingly clear. Theodora
greeted Henry with a genuine warmth that Zinzendorf had
never seen in her before. Wallowing slightly in the pathos of the
situation, he broke off the informal engagement and accepted
the situation as an expression of God's will and a chance to display some heroic gallantry.

Zinzendorf was undoubtedly familiar with the words of
Jesus when he said, "Give, and it will be given to you" (Luke 6:38),
and in Zinzendorf's case, those words came true in a most unexpected way. As he gritted his teeth and got stuck into his friend's
wedding preparations, he hardly noticed Reuss's charming and
capable sister Erdmuth Dorothea. But as their conversation
gradually moved away from caterers and seating plans, and a
friendship developed, the momentum proved unstoppable.
Eighteen months later, on September 7, 1722, Nikolaus Ludwig
von Zinzendorf and Erdmuth Dorothea Reuss were married.

In his soul-searching over Theodora, Zinzendorf had
done a lot of reflecting on what he was really looking for in a
marriage partner. He spoke of such matters in a letter, which
was far removed from the usual formalities, to his future
mother-in-law:

I foresee many difficulties in this case; as I am but a poor acquisition for any person, and the dear Countess Erdmuth must not only enter upon a life of self-denial with me, but also co-operate with me in my principal design, namely, to assist men in gaining souls for Christ, under shame and reproach, if she will be of any service to me.[6]

In Theodora, Zinzendorf would have chosen an entirely suitable candidate for the position of countess. In Erdmuth, he found much more. She was well equipped to handle the affairs of court and country estate, but she also genuinely shared her new husband's faith and his concern to put it into practical expression. She also had the financial and administrative talents that he himself frequently lacked. On several occasions during their life together, it was Erdmuth's careful stewardship that narrowly saved the count (and the movement he led) from financial ruin.

Faith Versus Law

If Erdmuth Dorothea wanted insight into her fiancé's priorities in life, it would not be long in coming. After his life-shaping encounter in the gallery at Düsseldorf, Zinzendorf was increasingly of the view that he should enter the service of the Lutheran Church. His family considered this to be beneath the dignity of a noble count.

In an age when birth counted for everything, young Lutz was destined for high position and royal service as a matter of inevitability. Finally, Zinzendorf reluctantly submitted to the wishes of his elders and accepted the post of king's counselor at the court of the wonderfully named Augustus the Strong of Saxony.

If he couldn't become a preacher of the gospel in the traditional way, Zinzendorf determined that he would use his position to do the next best thing. While at court in Dresden, he
started to hold meetings every Sunday afternoon, inviting anyone who would come to study the Bible and discuss spiritual
topics. Zinzendorf satisfied the initially suspicious clergy by
pointing out that Luther had permitted and encouraged
Christians to do exactly what he was now doing. Once it had
been proven that he was genuine and was not attempting to
start some kind of new sect, they became much more relaxed
and even held up the count as an example others might do well
to follow.

Back at home in the country, Zinzendorf bought his grandmother's estate at Berthelsdorf and had a new manor house
erected for himself and his future wife. For many people,
designing and building their own home is a lifelong dream and
a once in a lifetime challenge. Zinzendorf not only took the
process in his stride, but he also adapted the architectural
themes of his day to a less grandiose and more human scale,
pioneering the Moravian style, which was ultimately recognized as a genre in its own right. Above the door he had an
inscription carved that summed up his attitude to extravagant
displays of personal wealth:

> As guests we only here remain;
> And hence this house is slight and plain . . .
> We have a better house above,
> And there we fix our warmest love.[7]

In spite of his successes at Dresden, Zinzendorf was frustrated that genuine Christian fellowship seemed to be confined
to the wealthy in their drawing room meetings. He felt convinced that what was good for the nobles was also essential for

the common people. His plan for Berthelsdorf was a bold one: He would use his influence as lord of the manor to create a Christian community, which reflected the best ambitions of writers such as Spener, Luther and others.

One of his many powers was the right to appoint the parish priest, and Zinzendorf chose his friend and confidant John Andrew Rothe. He promised Rothe that he would offer him every support and would be directly and personally involved whenever his duties at court allowed. Zinzendorf introduced Rothe to the villagers, and at his induction service, Schafer, the Pietist preacher from Gorlitz, prophetically stated, "God will light a candle on these hills which will illuminate the whole land."[8] He would be proved right, although not perhaps in the way he might initially have expected.

With Zinzendorf unable to be at Berthelsdorf as often as he would have liked, he left the people in the care of Rothe and the estate itself in the hands of a wily steward named Heitz. Heitz continued the work on the new manor house, for which he recruited a number of craftsmen, possibly including a carpenter from Gorlitz by the name of Christian David.

The Bush Preacher

Christian David came with a remarkable personal history. He was brought up Catholic in neighboring Moravia but knew that he was lacking something. He became friends with some Protestants and was impressed by their willingness to accept suffering for their beliefs, but as he read works for and against Luther, he felt that both sides were somehow missing the point. In his testimony he said:

> At last I loathed the very name of Christ. I could not bear to mention it. I hated the sound of it; and would never

willingly have either read or heard it. In this temper I
left Moravia, and wandered through many countries,
seeking rest, but finding none.[9]

He turned to the Bible for himself and became convinced at
least that Jesus was the Savior of the world and the Bible was the
Word of God. He went to Berlin and joined a Lutheran congregation, but in his own judgment declared of himself, "My soul
was not in peace. . . . I now also led a very strict life. I read much,
and prayed much. I did all I could to conquer sin; yet it proved
not: I was still conquered by it."

He enlisted in the Prussian army, hoping that military life
would provide some space for him to clear his head, but it was
not to be. "Now I thought I should have more time to pray and
read, having with me a New Testament and a Hymn-book. But in
one day both my books were stolen. This almost broke my heart."

Following his discharge, he wandered from town to town,
knowing that he was looking for something but frustratingly
unsure of exactly what it was. Finally, at Gorlitz, he came into
contact with two Pietist clergymen named Schafer and
Schwedler, who seemed to have something of what he lacked.
He contracted a serious illness while in Gorlitz, and as he lay
close to death for over four months, Schwedler visited and
cared for him daily. This simple but profound expression of
God's love did what years of inquiry and argument had failed
to achieve. Christian David was finally able to declare, "Here I
found the peace I had long sought in vain; for I was assured my
sins were forgiven." When he was well, he settled in Schwedler's
church and was soon married.

If Christian David's personal searching was at an end, his
drive and passion were, if anything, now even greater. Although
settled in Gorlitz, every so often he would risk his life to cross
over into Moravia to tell his old friends of the joy and peace

that he had found. His preaching was simple, biblical and direct. He became known as the "bush preacher." Christian David came to a people who had been clinging to their beliefs under regular persecution for years. Their Bibles and hymnbooks were confiscated, some believers were imprisoned and others were tortured into confessing their allegiance to the Catholic authorities. Yet his words continued to stir the flames of faith back into life.

In an effort to aide these persecuted people, Christian David came up with a bold plan. He spoke to Pastor Schafer, Schafer introduced him to Rothe, and Rothe took him to Zinzendorf. Would the noble lord, Christian David asked, allow a group of these persecuted believers to come and settle on his lands, where they could live and worship in freedom? Zinzendorf was uncertain—the people would be coming without any references, and if they turned out to be a band of heretics they could upset his plans for the community at Berthelsdorf. On the other hand, he felt honor-bound by his oath "as a Knight of the Order of the Mustard Seed"[10] to grant them assistance. In the end, he gave his permission: If they came, then they would be allowed to stay.

Asylum Seekers

Christian David was delighted and headed back to Moravia to share the good news that he had found a place of refuge. In the village of Sehlen, two brothers by the name of Neisser, with their families, concluded that this was a door that had been opened by God. Leaving their homes and possessions, they set off on the dangerous trek across the mountains and into Saxony. The journey took them nearly two weeks, and they arrived weary and footsore with Christian David at their head on June 8, 1722.

Zinzendorf was away in Dresden, and the steward Heitz shrewdly reasoned that it might be best if the newcomers were settled away from the village until their credentials were better established. In any case, the Neissers were cutlers and knife grinders. The small village of Berthelsdorf would not give them enough trade to earn an honest living and they preferred to be positioned by the main road. He thus showed them to a small hill called the *Hutberg* ("watch-hill") about a mile away from the village. The scene was hardly inviting: The ground was damp, the road rutted, and water was not immediately available. Nevertheless, after their journey they were more than happy to set up camp in a derelict farmhouse and see what tomorrow would bring.

In spite of his initial caution, Heitz set about promoting the welfare of the refugees with enthusiasm. Lady Gersdorf provided a cow to give milk for the children. Heitz marked the trees that Christian David could cut down to provide wood for houses, and the carpenter started swinging axes around with his usual energy. The two men discussed their plans, and Heitz wrote to the count outlining what they had in mind: "May God grant that your Excellency may be able to build on the Hutberg a town which will live under the Lord's Watch, and whose inhabitants will keep the Lord's Watch day and night."[11]

The German word for "Lord's watch" is *Herrnhut*. The new settlement had found a name, and a second word of unrecognized prophecy had been released over the barely established community.

North of Dortmund
Wednesday, June 2, 2004, 15:30 GMT

With the weather front behind us and nothing but a few showers forecast between here and Dresden, Justin fancies his promised go at flying the plane. Like most small airplanes, Alpha Mike has full dual control. The panel is crammed with a bewildering array of instruments, but the process of learning to fly for the first time is strictly an eyes-outside-the-cockpit affair.

Justin settles his feet on the rudder pedals and both hands on the control yoke. He follows me through some basic maneuvers to get a feel for what does what. Then it's his turn. The sensitivity of the controls seems to take him by surprise. His knuckles go white as he grips the yoke harder, depriving him of the vital "feel" he needs to sense what the plane is doing. Having lost the freedom to exercise any natural stability, Alpha Mike enters a descending left turn. I take the controls back and we talk through the tricky balance between over controlling and under controlling.

The second go is much better. Justin holds us straight and level, and then pulls off a gentle turn in response to my navigational request. He's obviously relaxing into it, but darkening sky ahead interrupts our flying lesson. I start a slow descent, but the sky seems to be a solid wall of grey. Suddenly the cloud wall is lit up from inside by a bright flash of lightning. We are heading straight into a huge thunderstorm.

How we didn't see it sooner, I still don't know. Maybe the answer is that some things are just too big to see. This storm cloud is a monster. More than 10 miles across and 6 miles high, it doesn't just fill the sky; it *is* the sky. I turn Alpha Mike around and start to plan how we are going to detour around it.

To the north, the cloud wall looks solid. To the south it appears to curve away, so we are probably nearer the southern edge. Flying south will take us over the regional airport at Dortmund, so I select 134.17 and give them a call on the radio. Sometimes, just occasionally, even public officials go beyond the call of duty to be of help. The controller at Dortmund would be entirely within his rights to tell us to stay out of his airspace and sort out our own problems. Instead, he gives me an immediate clearance to track right over his airfield. He offers us a landing too, but I advise that we are going to divert round. He telephones ahead to Arnsberg, a few miles farther on, who confirm that they have clear skies and no thunderstorm in sight.

The detour has taken us south of our planned route. Ahead we can see a long, sinuous lake surrounded by low hills. A quick check of the map pulls me up with a shock of recognition: We are looking at the Möhne reservoir.

The Möhne dam passed into legend on the night of May 16, 1943, when it was breached by the "Dam Busters" of the RAF's 617 squadron. As a child, my father gave me his 1954 paperback account of the story, and I, the aircraft-mad kid, read its yellowing pages until the cover fell off. Now, with the dam only a few miles ahead, the connection with history is too strong to resist and I trim for a gentle descent.

Approaching from the west, we see the dam first. It is a stained, gray concrete monolith crowned by two low towers, once filled with murderous flak guns. Beyond it the two arms of the lake are separated by a wooded peninsula, across which the bombers came. Even to be here in an airplane feels like a violation of memories—of 133 young men who set out from England along a route very similar to our own, and only 77 who came back. We are here thanks to radio and satellite navigation and the gratefully received assistance of Dortmund air traffic control. Those other men flew at night with primitive navigation equipment and people shooting at them the whole way. A descending turn brings us low over the woods. Throttle wide, holding the nose down, speed builds to 115 knots, and Alpha Mike races across the surface of the lake toward the dam. Crossing the wall between the towers, there is a moment of vertigo as we soar out over the valley below. Its peaceful villages have probably changed little in 60 years. In the village of Himmelpforten (which means "heaven's gates") on that May night, Father Berkenkopf had been awakened by the first explosion and knew instantly what it meant. He ran to his small gray stone church and began to ring the bell, the signal he had arranged with the villagers. The bell rang out for 20 minutes as four successive explosions weakened the dam. It rang for several minutes more as the wall of water thundered down the valley, and was only silenced as the village of Himmelpforten and Father Berkenkopf's body were swept away. No one knows exactly how many lives he was able to save, but 1,300 died as the floods from the two breached dams swept on for 50 miles.[12]

Our destination at Herrnhut, just a couple of hours beyond Himmelpforten village, is powerfully symbolic of the spiritual closeness that existed between Britain and Germany in the eighteenth and nineteenth centuries. It dramatically impacted John Wesley and it inspired the great British missions movements that were to follow. For 200 years these two nations were in the forefront of sacrificially taking the love and message of Jesus Christ to the ends of the earth. This puts into even sharper relief the demonic forces that caused us to spend the first half of the twentieth century systematically slaughtering each other in the battlefields and cities and peaceful mountain villages of Europe. I suppose I know this in my head, but here above the valley, I sense God speaking it directly into my heart.

Zinzendorf didn't choose his encounter with God in the Düsseldorf gallery, and we didn't plan ours above the Möhne dam. As we climb away and turn toward Paderborn, we pray for the future of Britain and Germany. Our prayers seem as inadequate as they are necessary. Europe has spent 60 years striving to achieve reconciliation through diplomacy, treaties, alliances and currencies. Here I start to understand that only a deep repentance and forgiveness expressed and received before God will ever deliver the true healing and restoration we all seek.

CHAPTER 4

THE HIDDEN SEED

Unless a grain of wheat falls to the ground and dies, it remains only a single seed. But if it dies, it produces many seeds.

JESUS OF NAZARETH

As the refugees arrived on Zinzendorf's estate, and Christian David started chopping down trees to erect the first house at Herrnhut, the count had very little idea of exactly whom he was dealing with. He knew that they had come from Moravia, in the eastern part of the modern-day Czech Republic. The rulers of Moravia were aligned to the Catholic powers in Europe, and Zinzendorf assumed that the travel-weary people arriving on his lands were simply Protestants fleeing from persecution back home. In fact, he was dealing with something altogether different and much older—the last remnant of a spiritual revival going back over 300 years. Their story was a remarkable one, studded with extraordinary characters, violence, political intrigue and world-changing reform.

Once Upon a Time

In the early 1400s, Wenceslas IV (a rather less virtuous successor to the "good king Wenceslas" of Christmas carol fame) ruled from Prague, capital of the strategically important kingdom of Bohemia. The Bohemian people and language were Slavic in origin, but real power in the nation rested in the hands of the mainly German nobility. The lands, the universities and the church were all under German-speaking control, and this was a constant source of ethnic tension. It also meant that faith and spirituality in Bohemia were at a low ebb. With much of the priesthood unable even to speak the language of the people, the church was in equal measures corrupt and irrelevant.

If the Church in Bohemia was decadent, the Church in Europe at large was in crisis. The authority of the Pope had for centuries been the driving force in holding together the Catholic faith. Now, with factions striving for political supremacy and naming their own (often brutal and immoral) candidates as rival popes, all was in danger of falling apart. Against this background it is hardly surprising that people of good conscience began to ask some difficult questions of the Church they served.

In Bohemia, the leading voice was Jan Hus. Hus was born in 1369 into a poor Bohemian family. He was a shrewd young man and realized early in life that unless you were born into the aristocratic elite, your prospects were pretty bleak. About the only route for advancement available to a commoner was to enter the Church, so Hus joined the clergy initially to get out of the poverty trap and into an easy life. His sharp wits and charismatic personality gained him rapid promotion, and he eventually became rector of Prague University. This position gave him an insight into the spiritual and political state of the nation and, for the most part, he didn't like what he saw.

He was also exposed to the ideas of John Wycliffe, the controversial English Church reformer and Bible translator in whom he found spiritual camaraderie and hope. He saw that Wycliffe had made a stand on many of the issues that were close to his heart, including the degenerate state of the Church and the need for the common people to hear the Bible in their native language and to understand and experience faith for themselves. Wycliffe's followers (the Lollards or "poor preachers") had been suppressed during the Peasants' Revolt and his writings condemned as heretical by the Church authorities, but in Bohemia his teaching made a lasting impression on Hus.

Hus first turned his fire on the nobility, denouncing their vices and exploitation of the people. The king complained to the archbishop, who answered him by declaring that "Hus [was] bound by his ordination oath to speak the truth without respect of persons." Hus then rounded on the clergy, condemning their selfish laziness and lack of concern for those in their spiritual care. The archbishop had a "quiet word" with the king to get Hus to back off—and Wenceslas delightedly reminded him that "Hus [was] bound by his ordination oath to speak the truth without respect of persons." Score? Fifteen-all. Meanwhile, Hus widened his attacks to take in the German minority's dominance of the court, the Church and the university. Prague was frantic with a heady mix of religious renewal and Bohemian nationalism. Wenceslas was sympathetic and passed a regulation granting fairer representation in the governance of the university, but this only fanned the flames and was widely recognized among the people as a victory for Hus over the establishment.

Rising Fires

In spite of the nationalistic nerve he had touched, Hus's heart was still primarily set on religious reform. He preached the ideas of Wycliffe in clear and compelling terms, knowing that this set him on a direct collision course with the Church authorities. He wrote two books, condemning the sale of "indulgences" (forgiveness of sins in return for a payment to church coffers) and declaring that true faith consisted of an inward rightness before God. He understood rightness before God to be a gift that God alone could give, and that it could not be obtained merely by signing up with a church organization.

In 1415, Hus was summoned to a church council in the German town of Konstanz. He went under a letter of safe conduct from Wenceslas's powerful bother-in-law Sigismund, but the king rapidly proved unwilling or unable to keep his promises. Hus arrived expecting to defend himself at an enquiry, but the court, in fact, moved straight to final sentencing. Hus was accused of heresy for his genuine opinions and for a malicious set of false accusations too. His defense was shouted down and on the 6th of July he was dragged past a bonfire of his own books and there, by the banks of the Rhine, he was burned at the stake.

As soon as news of Hus's death reached Prague, Bohemia erupted into all-out civil war. The Hussite wars flared until 1434 and saw Bohemia split into a mass of religio-political factions, united only in opposing the crusade sent by Rome to bring them back in line. All claimed allegiance to the memory of Hus, but few showed any real grasp of his vision. The Utraquists combined conservative nationalism with some minor points of Hus's doctrine. The Taborites were radical social reformers, and under the gifted, blind general Ziska, were the most effective militarily. The Adamites and Chiliasts espoused a bizarre set of beliefs and practices. The Waldenses most complemented Hus's teachings, with an emphasis on simple, biblical Christianity that they had brought from southern Europe a few decades earlier.

Of all the factions, the Taborites fought with the most determination, held out for several years against overwhelming odds, and were finally massacred at the battle of Lipany. It was the Utraquists who made a deal with the Church of Rome and came back under Roman authority in return for limited local autonomy and some symbolic concessions relating to the holy communion. Thus, the nationalistic side of Hus's legacy was resolved for the time being, but the deeper spiritual aspects of his vision were left to three very different personalities to carry forward.

Writer, Speaker, Actor

The first was the mysterious Peter of Chelcic. He was educated but not a part of the establishment; he lived in the rural south. He was familiar with the Bible and the writings of Wycliffe, Hus and others, but was not himself a priest and was independent of the Church hierarchy. He hated war and its associated brutality. In fact, he came to prominence for opposing General Ziska's decision to take up arms in the Hussite cause. In a series of written works, he concluded that the whole system of religion and politics was rotten to the core. His condemnation was colorful, vigorous and incisively accurate. Peter's response was not to offer a systematic theology like that of Wycliffe or Hus, but to make a passionate plea for people to return to the simple faith of Jesus' early disciples. He had no desire to lead any kind of movement, but as the Hussite wars drew to a close, numbers of people started to gather together, read and debate his pamphlets, and identify themselves as his "followers."

If Peter was almost a recluse, then John Rockycana was an out-and-out populist. He became archbishop-elect of Prague in 1448, and straightaway began to preach in the city what his pen pal at Chelcic was writing in the country. Rockycana was a brilliant speaker and, at first, many looked to him as the one who would bring Hus's vision into being. However, for all his brave words, Rockycana was an establishment man and it became clear that when push came to shove, he was not going to put into practice what he so eloquently preached.

The task finally fell on the shoulders of a middle-aged ex-monk named Gregory. He was a minor noble, a friend of Peter, a nephew of Rockycana, and well respected for his character, spirituality and good sense. With a few others, he hatched a scheme that was simple but, in his day, virtually treasonable. He declared that if the state church was incapable of reform, they would have to walk away and start their own spiritual society founded on simpler and more honest principles. Rockycana was unwilling to make the break himself but was open enough to speak to the king, who gave permission for them to settle on his estate in the secluded mountain valley of Kunwald. By 1458, Gregory the Patriarch (as he became known) had been joined by a mixture of Peter's followers, sincere Waldenses and Adamites from the time of Hus, a few sympathetic Utraquist priests, and people of deep religious experience from all walks of life. Through this motley group, the society that would soon become known as the "Bohemian Brethren" was born.

The priests administered the traditional sacraments of the church including bread and wine, baptism and confession. Apart from that, the Brethren came to God directly for wisdom and guidance. They sought to hear from God through reading the Bible and praying, and they found that their prayers were answered. They organized themselves to teach the people, visit families in their homes and help the poor from within their own community. They appointed elders to oversee their affairs. Those who had come from high positions renounced further involvement in church or state. The Kunwald community worked for its living, bothered no one and hoped to enjoy a quiet life pursuing the favor of God.

Live and Let Die

If the Brethren had hoped that they would be left in peace, they were badly disappointed. "Live and let live" was a philosophy of the 1960s, not the 1460s. They couldn't win: If they expressed their views in public, they would be seen as political agitators; but if they kept them private, they would be suspected of plotting against the powers that be, which is exactly what happened.

Gregory came to Prague to speak to a student group. King George, worried about malicious rumors regarding the activities at Kunwald, sent in the bailiffs. The students were given a tip-off but decided to stand their ground. They and Gregory were marched off to prison and tortured on the rack as the most practical means of modifying their opinions. The students caved in and publicly swore allegiance to the state church, but Gregory was made of sterner stuff. Close to death, it was again the intervention of Rockycana that secured his release and return to Kunwald.

Although Gregory was released, persecution of the Brethren broke out in deadly earnest. King George ordered that all his subjects be Catholics or Utraquists (the local Bohemian equivalent), and leaders of the Brethren were arrested and executed. Kunwald was overrun, and the Brethren fled to the forests and mountains. For several years they lived rough, moving by night, reading their Bibles by firelight and praying until their knees bled. In all this time they never retaliated, never rebelled and never took up arms in self-defense. The state hunted them, but the people increasingly respected and sheltered them. The more they were persecuted, the more the quality of their lives and faith shone through and their numbers steadily increased. Finally, moved by a mixture of shame and sound advice that he was only creating martyrs to the cause, the king gave up and let them be.

Until that moment, the Brethren had been a hybrid—an independent religious community but with priests from the state Utraquist church. By 1467, it was clear that this position was unsustainable; however, to break away completely was a huge decision. After weeks of prayer and fasting, the decision was finally made. From a group of nine nominees, three were chosen (by drawing lots) to be the first ministers of what had now become the Bohemian Brethren Church. A sympathetic Waldensian bishop ordained them, and they established their own episcopal succession.[1]

Gregory died in 1473, his life's work done. The legacy he left the Brethren was one of deep faith, simple life, sincere devotion and suspicion of power, wealth and influence. For 150 years they were to continue as one of the more remarkable moves of God in Christian history.

Under a succession of hostile kings, the Brethren endured repeated persecution but never took up arms in their own defence.[2] They submitted to imprisonment, exile, or even death rather than deny their beliefs. They became pioneers of popular education, combining the spiritual and secular in a way that equipped people for life and faith, and never sought to make a distinction between the two. They produced a Bohemian translation of the Bible (the so-called "Kralitz Bible"), a succession of hymnbooks that taught their beliefs through the songs of the people, and a method of teaching children to read and to understand the basics of Christianity in their own homes.

The Brethren were disciplined in their conduct and moral character, and their integrity made them prosperous in freedom and won them friends and protectors in persecution. They declared their belief in justification by faith and the Bible as their source of authority a full 50 years before Martin Luther spoke out in Germany and started the Protestant Reformation. Their doctrine was always practical rather than dogmatic, and they were rarely dragged into theological arguments. Their belief in the grace of God was matched by their determination to prove it through a life of spiritual disciplines and good works.

During a period of European history when religious confession and political allegiance were inseparably linked, the Brethren grew from virtual extinction to a position in which a significant proportion of the population of Bohemia claimed allegiance to this radical and different understanding of what it meant to be a follower of Jesus Christ.

The final chapter in the struggle between the Protestant states and the Holy Roman Empire was the Thirty Years War, fought between 1618 and 1648. Hostilities started in Bohemia and resulted in the defeat of the Protestant armies by General Tilly at the Battle of White Hill, near Prague. The aftermath signaled the end for the Bohemian Brethren. Prince Lichtenstein first beheaded the leading nobles, and then Ferdinand II set about the merciless destruction of the Brethren Church. The people were imprisoned, raped, tortured, executed, massacred. Their books were burned, their property confiscated, their church buildings were taken over, and every trace of the Brethren faith was systematically erased. The population of Bohemia dropped from 3 million to 1 million, as refugees fled and the dead piled up in every town and village. Even their graves were desecrated, as if to wipe their very memory from history.

Into the Ground

The last bishop of the Brethren, Jan Amos Comenius witnessed the full horrors of the mid-seventeenth century. Comenius was a pastor and an educationalist, overseer of the Brethren school and church at Fulneck. As war gripped Bohemia, Ferdinand's troops arrived at Fulneck and brutally sacked the village. Comenius fled to the protection of Baron Zerotin at Brandeis, on the way grieving the loss of his wife and one of his children and the almost unspeakable horror and brutality of a nation descending into barbarism and chaos. For a while he took refuge and wrote a biting allegory called *The Labyrinth of the World*. In it, he described the darkness and degeneration of society and identified a return to the faith, hope and love of Christ as expressed in the best of the Brethren Church as the only possible cure for the madness.

Finally, even the influential Zerotin was unable to shelter the Brethren any longer, and the last band of refugees set out to cross the mountains into Poland with Comenius at their head. As they turned back for a final view of their native land, Comenius looked up to heaven and prayed. He asked that God would preserve a "hidden seed" that would one day grow and become a great tree once again. With these prophetic words echoing in their minds, they left Bohemia forever, the valleys falling silent with the final strains of their despairing marching hymn:

> Nought have we taken with us,
> All to destruction is hurled,
> We have only our Kralitz Bibles,
> And our Labyrinth of the World.

The exiles settled at Lissa in Poland, and Comenius embarked on the other aspect of his passion: the transformation of education. He pioneered a revolutionary approach to elementary education, dispensing with rote learning of Latin and harsh punishments, and replacing them with a highly visual style of teaching in the children's own language, which taught them to explore and understand the world. His *Orbis Pictis* was the world's first children's picture book. For older students, his approach to Latin was to teach by usage and example first, and by theory second. His textbook *Janua Linguarum Resarata* ("The Gate of Languages Unlocked") enabled thousands to master this tricky but vital common language of learning, diplomacy and science. His *Great Didactic* was a remarkable vision of the concept of universal education.

In recent times, Comenius was included among *Life* magazine's "100 most influential people of the millennium," and is frequently given the title "The Father of Modern Education." He would have been honored but disturbed at being identified as a pioneer of secular learning, because for him the separation was meaningless. He saw teaching the truth of Jesus Christ to future generations as the key to reviving the Brethren Church, and the reformation of education itself as the church's great gift to society. He once said, "What I have written for youth I have written, not as a teacher, but as a theologian."[3] He believed that education should equip a person to live a life that flourished in both material and spiritual terms.

After the fall of Lissa, the last great center of the Brethren in exile, Comenius never lost faith that God would somehow preserve the hidden seed. Some of his last works were a republication of the traditional disciplines of the Brethren and a virtual "time capsule," describing in simple questions and answers the beliefs and practices of his beloved church. This final document he dedicated to "the pious and scattered sheep of Christ, especially those at F., G., G., K., K., S., S. and Z."[4] The simple code represented the villages of Fulneck, Gersdorf, Gestersdorf, Kunewalde, Klandorf, Stechwalde, Seitendorf and Zauchtenthal. In these quiet backwaters across the border into Moravia, the last recognizable fragments of Comenius's hidden seed remained. They met secretively in barns at midnight, sang their Brethren hymns on mountainsides away from prying ears and buried their Kralitz Bibles in gardens for fear of discovery.

As Christian David crossed the border again and returned with a second band of Moravian refugees, this time the new families came from the village of Zauchtenthal. Even though Zinzendorf had no knowledge of Comenius's century-old code, he was about to undergo an encounter with the "hidden seed," which would change his life forever.

PADERBORN HAXTERBERG AIRFIELD, CENTRAL GERMANY
WEDNESDAY, JUNE 2, 2004, 17:00 GMT

Haxterberg is everything I had expected a small German flying club to be. Neat. Orderly. Friendly, in an efficient kind of way. In just under an hour, with a smattering of each other's languages and lots of smiling, we obtain fuel, coffee, the latest weather forecast and some very agreeable cakes. They seem surprised that we intend to push on to Dresden tonight (I keep forgetting that they are an hour ahead, which means that it is now 7:00 P.M. local time), but it has turned into a beautiful summer evening and there's really no reason not to continue on our way.

We meet one more isolated shower shortly after take-off, easily dodged, then it is clear, smooth air all the way. Up above 3,000 feet, the view extends for miles in every direction and the scenery drifts serenely below us. Only the airspeed indicator confirms that we are still slicing through the sky at 115 miles per hour.

There is something about high flight that inspires all but the most hardened of human spirits to pray. It has to do with a sense of presence and perspective: You could almost reach out and touch the land below, yet you see things without the claustrophobic restriction of vision that is felt at ground level.

Two months before his death in 1941, the Canadian Spitfire pilot John McGee (who was himself born into a missionary family in China) wrote his famous poem, which ends with these words:

I've topped the wind-swept heights with easy grace
Where never lark nor ever eagle flew—

And, while with silent lifting mind I've trod
The high untrespassed sanctity of space,
Put out my hand, and touched the face of God.[5]

I have discovered this truth during many flights whose specific purpose was to pray (with others) for my community and nation. I am not surprised that Justin feels it too. Our prayers flow easily. We have no shopping list of requests with which to pester God. We spend time in silence, seeking to perceive what is on His heart for places He knows as intimately as a precious child, but for which we have only a name on a chart. Out of this sense flow requests, declarations and occasionally tears.

To the northeast, the old university town of Halle is visible. It was here that Zinzendorf spent those six formative years of his early school life. The trail is growing warmer. Zinzendorf would have sailed past our departure point at Southend many times on his visits to England. He was familiar with the cities of Holland and the waterways of the Rhine. Halle, though, is home territory. Reluctantly we give Leipzig-Halle airport a call. We will be close enough that they will want to identify us on their radar (which they do), but that obliges us to keep half an ear open for them on the radio from now on. Competing voices: something from which we have enjoyed a merciful interlude for the last hour of our trip.

The southern outskirts of Leipzig slip by below us. Row upon row of oppressive, gray, communist-era tenement blocks. Most are now abandoned, and the occupants of the rest are those without the means to make this choice. Yet here, as so often in places where the world would rather turn its back and walk away, God is not silent. Our prayers are for hope and a future, and we sense that they come from a source beyond our own understanding.

Behind us the sky is reddening with the approaching sunset. Journey's end is within reach; our next radio contact will be Dresden. I flip the frequency and press the transmit button: "Dresden Tower, Golf Foxtrot Mike Alpha Mike." I've been waiting to say that all day!

"Golf Alpha Mike, Dresden Tower, pass your message."

"Golf Alpha Mike, a PA-28, Paderborn Haxterberg to Dresden, VFR, 3,000 feet on 1018, approaching Meissen to join via Whiskey, request joining instructions."

The momentous significance of first contact quickly subsides into the routine technical dialogue of a small airplane approaching a large airport. Below us the city is coming to life with thousands of lights in the gathering dusk. A few miles ahead there is an imposing complex of illuminated concrete buildings. The tower asks me if I have the airfield in sight. I reply, "Negative." It *can't* be that big . . .

But it is. The Saxon government is obviously taking regeneration very seriously, and Dresden's new airport terminal is a full-blown international facility. Alpha Mike slides self-consciously down the brightly lit approach path, and I try to decide which 10 percent of the runway we should land on to avoid having to taxi a mile to the apron. A minibus with an illuminated "Follow me" sign on the roof turns up to guide us to our stand. A marshaller jumps out, complete with fluorescent jacket, ear defenders and a pair of neon wands and starts giving us the full routine of hand signals. We both complete our assigned roles in the slightly comical charade of parking a plane that is no bigger than his van; then I pull back the mixture lever and Alpha Mike's propeller jerks to a halt. The marshaller inserts a set of chocks, which are four times wider than our front wheel. We're here.

The private aviation terminal is large, modern and deserted apart from one woman at a desk whose job is totally obscure but clearly doesn't involve talking to us. From here a door leads out into the public arrivals hall. We share the wood-and-chrome chairs with a couple of dozen people waiting for a delayed flight due in from Frankfurt. Half a continent away from home, I switch on my mobile phone and it manages to raise Markus Laegel at the first attempt.

Markus's apartment is in the Neustadt, which is the nightlife capital of Dresden and boasts over 500 cafés and bars. People are out everywhere, fueled by the restless energy of the city. Far too stoked from the day's events to sleep, we head for a Bierkeller and chat until 1:00 in the morning. It takes that long for our conversation to make the transition from journey to destination. Tomorrow we drive the final, short leg to Herrnhut.

CHAPTER 5

SUMMER OF '27

*The Moravians . . . marked one of the purest moves
of the Spirit in church history.*

JIM GOLL

S itting around the campfire in the gathering dusk of a summer evening, the new arrivals shared stories that made the heart pound and the spirit soar. From the tales they told, it was hard to disagree that God had been with them in their journeying. One (David Nitschmann) recounted how a rope had mysteriously appeared at the window of the tower in which he was a prisoner. Others (including another David Nitschmann) had stumbled against their prison door to find that the bolt was now loose. Yet another had walked out of a dungeon past armed guards in broad daylight without once being noticed.

Christian David traveled into Moravia on 10 occasions, each time bringing back more of the precious "hidden seed" to their newfound refuge at Herrnhut. The Austrian authorities had placed a price on his head, and even the safe house that he had been using had been flattened by their troops as a warning to others. In spite of this, he continued to cross the border undetected, and little bands of men, women and children continued to place their lives in his hands as they made the hazardous return trip across the mountains to safety.

Some of the Moravian exiles knew little of their heritage but had been stirred by the preaching of Christian David and others. The group from Zauchtenthal, though, was rather different. They still held on to the writings of Comenius, secretly used the Brethren hymns in their worship and longed for the day when the renewal for which he had prayed would occur. They had initially set out for Lissa in Poland, hoping to find survivors of the group who had been there 70 years before. At the urging of their guide Christian David, they agreed to pass through Herrnhut on the way to see what was happening there.

Birth of a Community

At the time of the Zauchtenthal Moravians' arrival in May 1724, the "town" was hardly impressive. A grand total of three houses had been started, and only one of those was finished. However, the scene was industrious and clearly had purpose to it. In the afternoon they discovered that a stone-laying ceremony for a new college was due to take place. The count and countess arrived and took an obvious interest in what was going on. Zinzendorf gave a speech full of vision and spiritual ambitions for the new institution. His old school friend Frederick de Watteville offered a fervent and passionate prayer, kneeling on the heavy cornerstone. The five leaders from Zauchtenthal were touched. They stayed, were added to Herrnhut's increasingly diverse collection of people, and became the heart of the Brethren community there.

The founding of the college and the presence of de Watteville were signs of the steady progress that Zinzendorf was making with his plans to create a "church within a church" at Berthelsdorf. The spiritual temperature was beginning to rise as matters of faith increasingly became an integral part of community life. Rothe preached in the village church on Sunday mornings with passion and insight. In the afternoon, Zinzendorf invited his tenants to the manor house to hear a practical application of the morning's sermon. Heitz led the villagers in Bible classes. The count also held meetings for prayer and singing in worship on summer evenings. Many of the villagers were receptive, and the church building had to be enlarged—a project that Zinzendorf was more than willing to fund.

Delighted, but still not content that he was reaching his tenants with the gospel, Zinzendorf also looked further afield. To maintain contacts with leading Christian thinkers, he made regular journeys to Halle and other centers of learning. To reach people beyond the borders of his own estate, he set up a printing press at Ebersdorf and started sending letters, pamphlets and affordable copies of the Bible in all directions. With all this activity going on, the presence of his friend and fellow Mustard Seed initiate Frederick de Watteville was a great support, and de Watteville enthusiastically shared Zinzendorf's aims and vision for the various projects.

With his energies occupied by the work at Berthelsdorf and his official duties at Dresden, Zinzendorf had largely ignored the growing community of Herrnhut. Word had quickly gotten around that the count was offering a place of sanctuary for persecuted Protestants, and as a result, a thoroughly mixed assortment of refugees, misfits and cranks had started to arrive at the village on the hill. Apart from requiring that they had to be fleeing from persecution and must be willing to offer their allegiance to the Lutheran Church, Zinzendorf basically let them be. The Moravian Brethren were still the largest group, but to them were added groups with Calvinist views, followers of the sixteenth-century reformer Kaspar Schwenkfeld, vague evangelicals, hardline Pietists, and all manner of others.

Divided We Stand

What happened next was sad but predictable: The people of the Herrnhut community began to fall out with each other.

The Moravians had a tradition of flexibility in doctrine, but they could only be pushed so far, and some of the other groups positively delighted in stirring up theological controversy. As Herrnhut rose out of its initial poverty to become an averagely prosperous village, the sense of community and mutual support ebbed away to be replaced with backbiting and competition.

Into this deteriorating situation came a gifted speaker and leader by the name of Kruger. He had been kicked out of the church at Ebersdorf following a dispute with the local priest, and in August 1726, he came to Herrnhut where he soon attracted a following. He spoke eloquently against the Lutheran Church in general and was particularly opposed to Zinzendorf and Rothe. Using images from the biblical book of Revelation, he dubbed Zinzendorf "the Beast" and Rothe "the False Prophet." Christian David was completely won over—his simple faith was swamped by Kruger's clever words and he withdrew completely from the count's work. Most of the Herrnhutters ceased to attend the church down in the valley at Berthelsdorf, and talked openly of starting a sect of their own.

For all his natural gifting, Kruger was in fact in the process of going out of his mind. His ravings became wilder and wilder, and eventually, he was confined to a lunatic asylum in Berlin. Unfortunately, by then the damage had already been done. By 1727, Herrnhut had turned from a quiet community of persecuted refugees into a mess of factions and intrigue. Christian David and John Rothe were no longer on speaking terms, and Rothe openly warned his villagers to keep away from the dangerous fanatics up the hill.

At the beginning of May 1727, Zinzendorf took extended leave from the court in Dresden and came back to Berthelsdorf to spend more time on his various projects. The situation at Herrnhut horrified him. In purely practical terms, it appeared that they were close to a breakdown of civil order. Spiritually, the atmosphere was a million miles from the kind of community Zinzendorf had hoped to build.

The Count must have been tempted to eject the warring factions from his property, but again acted in line with his commitment to be "kind to all men." With characteristic boldness, his first step was to move with his wife and young family out of their comfortable manor house and into an apartment within the newly constructed orphanage at Herrnhut. This placed him right in the heart of the troubled settlement. Countess Erdmuth initially found the move difficult, being unused to living in such close proximity with people from lower social classes, but Zinzendorf took to his new situation with remarkable ease. He had a natural approachability and was able to talk to almost anyone where matters of faith were concerned.

Intervention

As lord of the manor, 27-year-old Zinzendorf also had almost unlimited authority, which he now resolved to use to recover the situation. On the twelfth of May, he called a meeting of the entire community on the Hutberg. He had always been a compelling speaker and, with charged emotions, lectured for three hours on the state the community members had allowed things to get into and on the sin of division amongst fellow believers. Afterward, he produced a document of "Manorial Injunctions and Prohibitions" inspired by a book he had read, which described the community life of Jesus' first followers. As lord of the community, he was in a position to demand that the people submit to his regulations, and he did just that. He also proposed a number of "Statutes" that described a voluntary religious society based on submission to Christ and respect for one another, which he asked that they consider adopting as their basis for community life. At the end of the meeting, the settlers shook hands and agreed (not that they had much choice) to obey the new "Injunctions and Prohibitions."

Zinzendorf's judgment that Herrnhut needed a shock and an intervention of strong leadership had been incisively accurate. The atmosphere changed almost overnight, as if the village was waking up from a bad dream. Seizing the initiative, Zinzendorf set out to win back the key protagonists. He drafted a "Brotherly Union and Compact," which amounted to an agreement to forgive the horrendous things that had been said and done over the past couple of years and to live together in Christian brotherhood in accordance with the Statutes he had already proposed. He himself applied the first signature, effectively laying down his right to enforce retribution on his rebellious tenants. Christian David and the wise mediator Schafer were the next to sign. At a meeting on the fourth of July, virtually the entire community added their names to the compact and voluntarily agreed to live by the (not inconsiderable) demands of the statutes.

In spite of the vicious personal attacks that Christian David had made against Zinzendorf and Rothe, Zinzendorf was convinced from past experience that somewhere underneath Christian David's façade was the zealous, honest and good-hearted person he had first come to know. He gambled that the best way to bring David back to his senses was to give him some responsibility for sorting out the mess, and thus boldly announced that he was nominating David as one of 12 community elders.[1] Again, Zinzendorf's intuition was inspired. Christian David set about implementing the injunctions and statutes with all the vigor and energy he had shown before.

Brooding of the Spirit

By mid-June, something remarkable was happening in the village of Herrnhut. The place was a model of civic harmony and order. People who had previously been at each other's throats were meeting together in the evenings for prayer and praise. The count held meetings every day, which were enthusiastically well attended. Rothe's church was packed. Christian David persuaded the community to get to grips with what it really meant to live together in God's love by hosting meetings to study the first letter of John from the Bible. The atmosphere was brooding with a kind of benign spiritual intensity, yet it lacked any of the religious showmanship and emotional manipulation formerly employed by Kruger. In a few short weeks, Herrnhut had advanced to a state that Berthelsdorf had not yet seen despite five years of diligent effort. They could only attribute the events at Herrnhut to the grace of God.

By July, Zinzendorf was confident enough to leave the village on brief trips, although he found it hard to pull himself away from the sense of divine presence that seemed to hang over the place. On one trip away from the village, he read an old Latin manuscript that caught his eye. The book was Comenius's *Account of Discipline of the Brethren Church,* and as Zinzendorf read the old man's desperate appeal that their traditions should somehow be preserved, the *Pfennig* finally dropped. He realized that he had become the guardian of the last remnant that Comenius had prayed would one day be restored. Even more remarkably, the disciplines recorded by Comenius bore a startling resemblance to the Statutes he himself had drawn up only a few weeks earlier. As he read, Zinzendorf knew that God was again speaking to him, only this time through the words of an old book. In characteristically impulsive style, he determined that he would expend his fortunes, and if necessary his life, to preserve and restore the hidden seed that God had placed in his hands.

Returning to Herrnhut, he read extracts from the book to the assembled community. For the Moravians the impact was momentous. They had come to Herrnhut simply as another step on a long journey of exile. Now, just as a spiritual revival seemed to be breaking out around them, God had moved this foreign count to throw the considerable weight of his personal resources behind their cause too. They were excited, but at the same time must have been aware that they were becoming caught up in a current even bigger than the century-old dreams they had held on to and preserved.

Singularity

In the first week of August, Pastor John Rothe felt inspired to call the whole community together for a special celebration of holy communion in honor of the bond of love and goodwill that now existed between them. As the people from Herrnhut walked the mile down the hill into the village, on August 13, 1727, they urgently reassured one another of their forgiveness for past upsets and declared their newfound goodwill toward each other. The sense of expectation was intense, and no one was willing to go into the event personally unprepared or harboring any old hurts or sense of guilt. As they entered the door of the church at Berthelsdorf, the hairs on the backs of people's necks started to rise. The atmosphere was electric. Everyone knew that something was about to happen, but no one was quite sure what it was.

Jesus' first disciples had gathered in an upper room, and at Pentecost they experienced an encounter with the Holy Spirit, the living presence of God. As Zinzendorf began a prayer of confession in the small church at Berthelsdorf, the pregnant heavens over Herrnhut finally burst open and the power and glory of God descended on the assembled people. The sense of God's presence went off the scale—beyond words, beyond description, beyond understanding. Every account struggles and fails to convey adequately the experience the two communities shared. The Spirit of God came like a windstorm: mighty, rushing, irresistible. The love and holiness of God touched the people like a firestream: heart-warming, dangerous, life-branding.

The reality of the experience was undeniable. Even as far away as Hungary, Christian David and Melchior Nitschmann (who happened to be away traveling) were overcome by an overwhelming impulse to pray. On their return, the first question they asked was, "What was happening at 10:00 A.M. on the morning of the thirteenth of August?" They were amazed, but somehow not surprised, to discover that they had been touched by the Spirit of God at exactly the same time as the outpouring in Berthelsdorf, of which they had been completely unaware.

As the people walked back up the hill to Herrnhut, what now separated them from the journey they had made earlier that morning was an encounter with eternity. The irresistible love of God had flowed out of that breach and impelled them to a renewed fellowship with Christ and with each other. The Herrnhut diary for that day encapsulates the life-changing nature of the events of August 13:

> Those who previously could not tolerate one another now stood in the graveyard in front of the church and embraced, swearing promises of true friendship; and so the whole congregation came back to Herrnhut as new-born children.[2]

What started as spiritual rebirth in the hearts of individuals was soon to manifest itself in the transformation of the entire community.

Dresden Neustadt

Thursday, June 3, 2004, 08:30 local time

Breakfast with Markus consists of bread rolls and jam. And black bread with ham and cheese. And scrambled eggs with sausage. And orange juice. And coffee. And fruit. Clearly an enthusiasm for breakfast is a unifying factor between our two cultures. There is also a jar of Robertson's mincemeat bought in Spain on the understanding that it was a British delicacy; however, they have found it to be strangely unrewarding when spread on toast. Justin and I spend a hilarious few minutes trying to explain about mince pies.[3]

Our transport to Herrnhut is to be a borrowed old blue Volkswagen Polo. One of its wing mirrors is rather prominently hanging off (goes with the territory in the Neustadt). Five minutes with a new reel of silver gaffer tape fixes that one, and we squeeze into the car and hit the road.

The first leg out of Dresden is a spacious autobahn to Bautzen. The wing mirror is still holding on at motorway speeds. Turning off, we head south down the country roads toward Herrnhut.

The two people I know who have been here have offered me the same disclaimer regarding Herrnhut: "Don't expect anything special; it's just an ordinary German village." In some ways, they reassured me, that is the point. If God could move in such a remarkable way here, then He can do it anywhere. In fact, as the bright yellow village sign finally appears around a bend in the road, I feel a surge of excitement—probably something to do with having battled the elements across half a continent to get here. In these days of mass transportation, we forget the effect that our journeying can have on how we encounter our destination. We park next to an admittedly very ordinary public sports field and get out.

First stop is the Moravian archive and library. Markus has phoned ahead and the archivist, Rudiger Kruger, meets us. He leads us upstairs to the Zinzendorf room. The furniture and surroundings are evocatively eighteenth century. On the walls there are portraits of famous figures from the Zinzendorf family and the Herrnhut community. Herr Kruger lifts the cover off the table at which we are sitting—underneath it is very clearly the same one around which the count and others are depicted in one of the 250-year-old paintings.

Kruger leaves us and returns with a box containing a small velvet-covered card. Mounted on it are some of the items we had been hoping to see: an immaculately enameled medallion and five small golden rings, the original insignia of the Order of the Mustard Seed. On the rings, the Greek inscription ("None of us lives for himself") is clearly visible, again enameled rather than engraved. Herr Kruger seems excited too. He has only been working here for a year, and in that time no one has yet asked to view these items, so this is the first time he has ever seen them. They are not sure exactly who owned each of the rings, beyond the fact that they were formerly the property of the Zinzendorf family. It is quite possible that one of them belonged to the count himself. What stories could this piece of jewelry tell? Of storm-lashed crossings over the Atlantic to the West Indies and Pennsylvania in square-rigged sailing vessels? Of stately visits to the kings and queens of Europe? Of long evenings in simple homes, sharing the love and grace of God with folk both receptive and hostile? Of a day in August 1727 when an encounter with the presence of God changed the destiny of this village forever?

We spend a long time looking at the rings. There is a sense of personal connection here, which makes it hard to pull ourselves away. Finally, we ask if we can pray. Herr Kruger is evidently more used to dealing with academics and researchers and appears slightly nonplussed, but we go for it anyway, keeping it simple and dignified.

Downstairs in the reading room, we complete a comprehensive registration form. "What is the purpose of your visit? (Please tick one of the following.)" I end up ticking "Research (book)" and "Personal interest," neither of which seems to do our presence here justice. They don't have a box for "Wild goose chase (neo-Celtic variety)."[4]

In two brown archive folders, we find a treasure trove of original documents relating to the Order of the Mustard Seed: the first covenant made by the "Confessors of Christ" in Zinzendorf's own handwriting and signed by himself and his four schoolfriends, dated "Anno 1716"; the neatly printed Büdingen edition of the rules from 1740, whose publication was caused by the death of the unfortunate Abraham von Rumswinkel; a couple dozen letters between members of the order, the paper carefully preserved, the copperplate script meticulous and formal.

We don't have time to fully review everything that is here. One letter especially catches our eye, mainly because it is written in English, and Justin and I stand a fighting chance of understanding it. Dated April 22, 1743, James Hutton (a close friend of Zinzendorf's in England) describes how this day he welcomed "Mr Erskine" (a Scottish member of parliament) into the order. Having "raised it at first as the motto of the ring made manifest," he goes on to explain in detail what the order involves and invites Erskine to join with them.

Erskine expresses a desire "to be in any shape useful in the kingdom of our dear Lord and saviour; at the same time declaring that he look'd upon this, as a greater honour done to him than any honour which could have been conferr'd upon him, by any Prince of Europe, or by them all together. He prayed to the Lord to help him, put it on the little finger of his left hand,

and kissed the ring, with much respect."[5]

Part of me (the slightly sad amateur historian part that I didn't realize I possessed) could happily stay here for the rest of the day. My ability to understand and relate to this compelling move of God in history has undoubtedly been strengthened by the many hours spent reading and studying, and this place takes that to a whole new level. The other part (the hungry, wild-goose-chasing part) reflects on that history and cries out with the Old Testament prophet Habakkuk:

> LORD, I have heard of your fame;
>> I stand in awe of your deeds, O LORD.
> Renew them in our day,
>> in our time make them known;
> in wrath remember mercy (Hab. 3:2).

The Habakkuk impulse wins out. We say our thanks and head up toward the Hutberg, the place where it all began, to see what else God has in store on this journey of revelation.

CHAPTER 6

PRAYER IGNITION

Here I continually met with what I sought for:
living proofs of the power of faith.

JOHN WESLEY

O n April 9, 1945, the Nazi concentration camp at Flossenburg was in uproar. Rumor had it that the advancing American army was only a few miles away. Communications had just been received from Himmler in Berlin, and detachment of the feared SS Black Guard came to the cell of a quiet intellectual pastor and theologian named Dietrich Bonhoeffer. He had already been held in various prisons for two years, his crime being to encourage Germans—by both his teaching and his example—to oppose the Nazi philosophy.

As Bonhoeffer was led away, his last known words, whispered to a fellow prisoner, were "This is the end. For me, the beginning of life."[1] He never saw the liberation of Flossenburg. Among the few possessions left in the cell was a small and well-thumbed book entitled *Losung* (literally "Watchword"). This simple book contains verses from the Bible chosen for each day of the year and had been a regular source of comfort and inspiration to Bonhoeffer during his imprisonment.[2] In the front, as had been done every year since the first printing in 1731, was a brief dedication written from the book's home of origin: Herrnhut.

The *Losung*, or "Daily Texts," is read today by 1.5 million people in over 50 languages. It is just one small part of a spiritual legacy that makes Herrnhut rank as one of the most remarkable examples of Christian community in modern history.

Heartbeat of Prayer

Following the unprecedented season of grace in the summer of 1727, which culminated in the spiritual outpouring of the thirteenth of August, the question in many minds must have been, "What's going to happen next?" It is an unfortunate fact that profound spiritual experiences do not always lead to lasting transformation in an individual or a community. However, Herrnhut had in its favor a positive and determined attitude toward spiritual formation. This was partly thanks to Zinzendorf, who had led a strong personal devotional life since childhood, and partly to the Moravian refugees, who were descendants of the old Bohemian Brethren and for whom discipline was the backbone of their church tradition.

The foundations of the spiritual disciplines include prayer, worship, and reading and applying the Bible. On August 27, just two weeks after the "Moravian Pentecost," a group of 24 men and 24 women entered into a solemn commitment to cover every hour of the day and night in continuous prayer.[3] What none of them could have realized was that Herrnhut would go on to pray continuously for 100 years.

The initial reason for starting the prayer watch was a sense that they were about to experience a backlash of spiritual opposition. Five days earlier, the Herrnhut *Journal* had recorded the following:

> We have been considering how necessary it is, for the well-being of the church, to keep constant watch over her—the church still being young in years and having an old enemy in satan, who rests neither by day nor

by night. To this end we have resolved to ignite a free-will offering of intercession in our town, which can burn day and night. We are contenting ourselves, however, with first putting the matter forward for consideration and allowing the Lord to stir the hearts of the brothers.

The focus was firmly on *intercession*—prayer for the needs and blessing of others. Participants were reminded that they had the whole rest of the day to pray for themselves! Individuals were allocated one-hour slots, and in principle they were to pray in their own homes, although in a tight community such as Herrnhut, people frequently met up to share the load together. In their own words:

> They prayed for individual souls, for pilgrims and missionaries in the Lord's service. They cried out to God for their nation, for its leaders and teachers. Finally, they lifted up the whole of Christendom and all mankind so that this institution of round-the-clock prayer would allow there to be no silence before the Lord day and night.[4]

There were soon 1,200 specific names on the list for prayer. Christian David noted that these included "many who were oppressed and in prison who told us of their needs and placed their situations in our hands. Also, many others who were working for the gospel, those who wished to join our fellowship, many who were ill or under attack and those who were struggling with repentance came to us for prayer."

The prayer watch was certainly not an abstract exercise in learning to cope with life's problems by offering them to God. The people of Herrnhut expected and saw real and tangible

answers to many of their prayers. One participant confident-
ly wrote:

> Various gifts and spiritual powers manifested themselves
> in the church at Herrnhut, and, in particular, many
> miraculous cures. Its members believed . . . the words
> which the Saviour spoke regarding the hearing of prayer;
> and when any particular affair pressed itself upon them,
> they spoke with Him concerning it . . . and it was done
> unto them according to their faiths.[5]

In addition to the hourly prayer watch, there was a frequent
practice of holding night watches, in which groups would meet
together and pray through the night. Christian David observed
that "the night-time hours are blessed hours because the nature
of man is lazy and sluggish, while the enemy is always active and
hard at work. The children of God must therefore call each other
regularly to watch and pray." This was distinct from the civic
night watch, whose main purpose was practical security.

Those whose prayer lives are restricted to occasional
organized meetings and private moments of need may struggle to comprehend the idea of praying continuously even for a
week. Anyone who has been personally involved in a venture of
this type will start to relate to the long hot days, freezing
nights, attacks of illness, pressures of work and family life, and
the dozens of other obstacles that the Herrnhut community
faced. For a community of around 100 people to pray every
hour of every day for a week is a challenging (but incredibly
rewarding and liberating) experience.[6] To keep it up for 100
years is awe-inspiring.

The fire at the heart of Herrnhut had been lit. The high-
voltage jolt of the thirteenth of August had not just led to a momen-
tary twitching, but to a strong, sustained heartbeat. From this

point onward, everything that happened was born, shaped, nurtured, released and supported in prayer. The covenant of 48 rapidly expanded to embrace the whole community. A weekly meeting soon followed to share encouragement and prayer needs. As messengers from Herrnhut started to move out into Europe and across the world, their letters home were read out and their situations offered up to God in an unbroken chain of prayer.

Rhythm of Worship

If the heartbeat of Herrnhut was prayer, then its breath was a rhythm of worship. Every day began with singing at sunrise in a short service known as the "morning blessing." At eight in the morning and eight at night, the community met together in the village hall for worship, prayer and reading from the Bible. The central feature of these meetings was music, and their theme was the "adoration of the Lamb."[7] Zinzendorf himself wrote hundreds of hymns (the contemporary worship music of the day), and because of his influence, others felt encouraged to do the same. The singing normally started with complete hymns, but frequently flowed into a spontaneous time of worship, blending together lines and verses to create an improvised and personal song of praise.

This rhythm of worship was not restricted to "holy days"; it was the normal routine, which ensured that every working day began and ended in praise. On Sundays, virtually the entire day was given over to various manifestations of worship. Around 5:00 A.M., singing began. From 6 o'clock to 9 o'clock, various adult groups held their own morning gatherings. A children's meeting took place at 10 o'clock, followed at 11 o'clock by the "official" morning service in the Berthelsdorf parish church. At 3:00 P.M., visitors and those who had been unable to get to the morning service could hear a repeat of the day's sermon given by the count or one of the other Brethren. At 4 o'clock there was an afternoon service at Berthelsdorf. At 8 o'clock the "normal" Herrnhut evening meeting took place, and finally, at 9:00 P.M. the young men would march around the village singing hymns and generally rounding the day off as it had begun.

It was at one of the evening singing meetings that the idea of the "watchword" first came about. Zinzendorf felt that a verse of Scripture that had been read out loud was of particular relevance to the community, so the following morning he passed the Scripture passage around from house to house so that everyone could reflect and meditate on it during the day. The choosing of a watchword for each day soon became a consistent pattern, and Zinzendorf and the elders established a system of collecting encouraging or challenging Bible verses and drawing one at random for the following day.

The German name *Losung* carries the ideas of a watchword, password or rallying cry; the daily text was all of these things. It ensured that the whole community shared a common focus on the Bible. The watchword became a bond of unity and a source of encouragement and direction, both for major decisions and in the everyday events of life. In 1730, the texts for the whole of the next year were drawn in advance and printed up as the first daily textbook. The Moravian textbook has been in print continuously from 1731 to the present day.[8]

Living on Purpose

According to the old Brethren tradition, worship was to be expressed in practical service. Brethren spirituality embraced the whole of life and refused to recognize a spiritual/secular division. Herrnhut embodied this holistic spirituality; they had elders to provide spiritual leadership and direction, visitors to encourage individuals in their homes, and monitors to administer practical discipline.

The people were organized to participate in the prayer watch and the worship meetings, but every practical need of the community was also met. There were groups appointed to maintain the village, teach the children, nurse the sick and help the poor. Every adult male, regardless of social status, took turns on the night watch. A court of justice oversaw agricultural and commercial matters and acted as arbiters in case of disputes. A town council was responsible for civic affairs, and a church council oversaw formal religious issues (Herrnhut was still officially a voluntary religious society operating within the state church). In theory, Zinzendorf held ultimate authority by virtue of his rank and position. In practice, his willing delegation and the sheer breadth and depth of involvement meant that the whole set-up was pioneeringly democratic in operation.

The numerous roles were well organized and filled in accordance with spiritual gifting and maturity rather than social position or rank. As a result, the duties and composition of the various teams changed frequently, based on needs and the availability of the "right" people for the task. If there did not appear to be anyone practically or spiritually qualified to fulfill a particular role, it was adapted or abolished rather than administered by the "wrong" person for the job. This charismatic approach to leadership was even more remarkable because it developed in the context of a feudal estate within a deeply hierarchical society. A day in the life of potter Martin Dober provides an example:

> At five he led the congregation in morning worship in the chapel of the orphanage. In attendance were some distinguished and learned people. At nine o'clock he might be visited by a count, a nobleman, or a professor,

who found him barefoot in his shop. For him that was quite proper. They seated themselves before his potter's wheel and paid heed to his words. That was an expression of the Holy in old Herrnhut.[9]

Trades and industries were actively encouraged, with the objective of providing for the community and generating a profit to support missions and outreach. Many crafts and businesses proved extremely successful in this respect, and one (Dürninger & Co.) eventually grew to become an international concern. No one could set up a business without the approval of the elders; ventures that wasted effort by competing with what was already plentiful or that could not be shown to be of practical and spiritual benefit were not allowed. The elders also exercised control over external influences on the state of the community. They placed restrictions on anything from traveling entertainers and peddlers, to repeating superstitions and telling "old wives' tales."

Herrnhut, contrary to its appearance, was not a commune. Individuals continued to own property and profit from their own trades. However, the universally accepted rule was that every member would keep to the same simple standard of living, and that any surplus produced would be given to the needs of the community or its wider missions and projects.

The means of enforcement were pastoral rather than legal. There was no complex system of taxes or financial allocations, but simplicity of lifestyle and generosity with wealth were regarded as basic requirements of spiritual health in an individual. As one of their leaders put it:

> To say that believers should have no personal property, but must have everything in common would be to go too far. But believers are to lay down their lives for one another and if it is needed not withhold property from others.[10]

Twentieth-century communism aimed for equality and communal ownership in theory but fell far short in practice. Herrnhut, with its voluntary participation based on personal conviction, achieved it in practice without the theory. There was no trace of consumerism and also no excessive glorification of community-ism for its own sake. Modern commentators have sometimes examined the community as a form of social experiment, but to Zinzendorf this would be missing the point. The similarities to the first biblical community of believers described in Acts 2:42-47 are remarkable. Everything flowed from shared expression of deep individual commitment to Christ, and as a result Herrnhut did not have the dehumanizing qualities of a system driven by social ideology.

Banding Together

At the most basic level, virtually every community member was part of a same-sex group of about three people, known as a "band." The bands met regularly (often daily) for prayer, encouragement, fellowship, accountability and confession. No one was exempt, as an extract from Zinzendorf's diary for 1729 shows:

> July 12: David Nitschmann and Christian David were at my table. We took stock of ourselves and told each other what yet remained to mar the image of Christ. I let them tell me first what I lacked and then I told them what they lacked.[11]

For worship and Bible teaching, the people met together in larger groups of about a dozen, known as "classes." Zinzendorf was tireless in moving among these small groups and would speak, worship or pray with people of all ages and situations, though he had a special heart for working with children.

The most comprehensive fusion of collective spirituality, communal life and personal commitment was probably the development of the "choir" system. In February 1728, a group of unmarried men moved into a house that soon became known as the "Single Brethren's house." The group already had a strong sense of camaraderie, which moving into a shared dormitory only served to heighten. The house was more than a living accommodation; it also served as a venue for their meetings, a workshop for crafts and a training school for apprentices.

The group eventually became known as the "Single Brethren's choir" (not surprising considering the amount of singing they seem to have done!), although their organization stemmed from much more than music. Over the next few years, other social segments followed their example. In 1730, 18 young women formed a "Single Sisters' choir" along the same lines. After casting lots, the leadership position was assigned to a 15-year-old peasant girl named Anna Nitschmann. Zinzendorf initially struggled to accept the idea that one so young with no formal training could take on this kind of responsibility, but what Anna lacked in experience she amply made up for in spiritual maturity and determination. Not only did she prove to be an inspirational leader of the Single Sisters, she would later go on to become one of the central figures in the whole Moravian movement.

Eventually the entire community was divided into ten "choirs" as follows: married couples, widowers, widows, the Single Brethren, the Single Sisters, older boys, older girls, young boys, young girls, and infants. Each group had their own leaders, and each held their own special services and festivals.

The choir system shaped the character and mission of Herrnhut in many ways. From a purely practical point of view, the emphasis on communal living meant that resources were shared efficiently and that a simple but adequate standard of living was enjoyed by all. Herrnhut simply did not suffer from the blighting poverty or excesses of wealth that were common across eighteenth-century Europe.

The choir system also served to release individuals for service in outreach or mission. In the society of the day, marriage was the immediate and only option for girls reaching the age of maturity (around 15), or young men completing their education or apprenticeship and wishing to start a home. The Single Brothers and Single Sisters committed together that marriage would be relegated to second place, behind serving the call of God in whatever form it came. Due to the freedom and mutual support of the choir "family," these two groups would become the driving force behind the explosive expansion of Moravian mission and renewal in the decades that followed. None of them took vows to remain single for life, and most of them did eventually marry, generally after the pattern of an individual's work and calling had begun to unfold.

For couples who felt called to travel and to work away from Herrnhut, often in mission fields that would have been difficult and dangerous for children, the choirs offered a secure environment in which to care for and educate children whose parents were absent. Individuals also left their partners behind for a period, which would have been impossible without the practical and emotional support the choirs offered.

The division into self-led single-sex groups meant that Herrnhut developed a formidable body of female leadership, in an age when society was male dominated at almost every level. Again, however, the community had no developed philosophy of female liberation and did not attempt to challenge cultural norms head-on. Instead, they insisted that both men and women were equally in receipt of Christ's mercy on the cross. It naturally followed, then, that both should give their lives to serving God to the fullest possible degree.

The Single Sisters' choir also allowed women to develop an independent "career" (spiritual or practical) without the social pressure to become a full-time homemaker. Their dress was conservative (the women all wore similar and simple outfits with only a colored ribbon to indicate their marital status), but their achievements were radical. Freedom of personal choice was not the point at issue, but allowing individuals freedom to respond to the calling and gifting of God on their lives certainly was.

Despite so much order and discipline, so much focus on service and devotion, the community at Herrnhut also celebrated as wholeheartedly as they served.

Join the Party

The traditional country pursuits such as drunkenness, coarse joking and minor acts of violence were discouraged at Herrnhut, but a whole collection of alternative traditions arose to take their place.

Once a month, the entire community came together for "congregation day," which was both an opportunity for fellowship and a chance to hear news from friends and relatives farther afield. Their gatherings were always filled with music and singing, and when they sang it was loud and proud. The community wrote literally thousands of hymns, and the instrument of choice for accompanying their worship was usually the trombone!

Each of the choirs also celebrated festivals and feast days of relevance to their particular group. One tradition the Single Brethren started, which was soon adopted by the rest of the community, was the so-called "love feast," or *agape*. This was a simple meal (initially rye bread and water, later white bread and tea), shared as a celebration of both friendship and spiritual unity. In practical terms, it presented an opportunity for socializing and conversation. It carried strong echoes of the meals of covenant that Jesus shared with His disciples, but it was in no way considered a replacement of the sacrament of Holy Communion. The love feast has continued into modern times, and has also spread to other denominations as a sign of unity that avoids the risk of theological controversy.

Even in death, for Herrnhut, sadness was tinged with joy and celebration. At the top of the Hutberg was a cemetery known as "God's Acre," which reflected the nature of their community in life. The dead were laid to rest according to their choirs, the companions with whom they had lived out their lives. Graves were marked with simple but dignified flat stones—the same type was used whether the occupant was rich or poor, of the nobility or the common people.

Funerals reflected both the sorrow of mourning and the very real celebration that another had gone to be with the Lamb whom they had so faithfully served. One grieving father (a simple tailor) once said of his son's death:

> Praised be the Lord, never better. He has taken the soul of my child to himself. I have seen, according to my desire, his body committed to holy ground. And I know that when it is raised again, both he and I shall be ever with the Lord.[12]

Whereas some people both then and now may find these words of absolute conviction in the face of bereavement almost too much to swallow, all the evidence supports them as heartfelt and genuine. Just before sunrise on Easter morning, the entire village would go up to God's Acre and, with choir and trombones, celebrate the resurrection of Christ while looking ahead to the resurrection of their comrades who had died in his service.

Herrnhut was not a perfect community, but it was a genuinely remarkable one and offers a fascinating prototype in social, human and spiritual terms. It explores and challenges many burning issues: cells and community living, accountability, sustainable lifestyles, the elimination of poverty, social justice, women in leadership, singleness, personal identity, holistic spirituality, global vision and mission, even our taboos surrounding death. We have since lived through over two centuries of "progress," yet it is hard to find a more relevant or challenging contemporary example to inspire us.

People came to Herrnhut from all over Europe. One of the early construction projects was a guesthouse to provide for the numerous visitors who wanted to experience this remarkable community for themselves. The Sunday afternoon "guest service" began in an effort to strike a balance between the need for close-knit internal relationships and opportunities for outsiders to be included in what was happening. Many guests left carrying Herrnhut's contagious brand of faith with them.

Zinzendorf was never satisfied with achieving a revival of faith solely within the borders of his own estates, no matter how remarkable or profound. Since childhood he had heard tales of missionary pioneers taking the message of Christ to lands across the seas. With The Mustard Seed covenant, he had committed "to send the gospel to the world." His enthusiasm brought direction to the spiritual imperative that always seems to flow from a profound encounter with the presence of God. In 1728, following a congregation day meeting at which the subject of missionary work in Turkey, Ethiopia, Greenland and Lapland had been discussed, 26 of the Single Brethren banded together into a mission prayer group. Each of the 26 members vowed that he would be ready to go "when the call came." They would not have long to wait.

HERRNHUT
THURSDAY, JUNE 3, 2004, 14:00 LOCAL TIME

Returning to the VW Polo, we discover that the midday sun (or maybe the local teenagers) has managed to achieve what an hour on the autobahn could not, and the wing mirror is hanging off again. A more obtrusive but hopefully sturdier job with the gaffer tape gets it back in position. Street legal once again, we head out of the village and up the gentle rise to the top of the Hutberg.

The Moravian cemetery, or God's Acre, in Herrnhut has got to be one of the most remarkable places I have ever visited. The first thing that strikes me is the scale. This is no village churchyard; the place must be the size of a couple of football fields. The layout is ordered and rectilinear, with plots divided up by neatly tended walkways and precisely spaced rows of lime-green trees. Between these are row upon row of identical headstones, each laid flat to the ground and inscribed with the names and details of those who have been laid to rest here.

A brief look at some of the inscriptions reveals the unity and diversity of this remarkable community. Members of the nobility are buried next to humble craftsmen, their gravestones identical, with only the names giving away their former status. Some have testimonies indicating that they had lived or died as missionaries to the farthest corners of the earth. Almost all end with a Bible verse or a simple, sincere prayer of hope.

In postmodern, post-Christian Europe, graveyards can be confusing places. Symbols of faith abound, but the words that have been chosen tell a story of lives lived without any kind of eternal context. I know of one headstone engraved with a picture of a Ford Mondeo, presumably the owner's most prized possession. There is something poignant but profoundly empty about a life defined by the ownership of a family saloon car. Here on God's Acre, it is evident that every person has lived and died in the knowledge and love of God. The hope of resurrection and eternal life seems to shine through every word engraved on the weathered slabs.

A few of the graves are marked with small wooden signs that we soon realize identify the more "famous" members of the Herrnhut community. Here is Christian David, whose vision and tireless energy were instrumental in bringing the community into being. There are others, men and women, whose names have gone down in Church or missionary history. In the center is the Zinzendorf family plot. Their memorials still lie flat, but they are larger and slightly raised—an accurate reflection of a man who gave his life to serving others but remained forever the count, living in equality but always first among equals.

In reference to those who have lived the life of faith before us, the Bible says:

> Therefore, since we are surrounded by such a great cloud of witnesses, let us throw off everything that hinders and the sin that so easily entangles, and let us run with perseverance the race marked out for us (Heb. 12:1).

Among the last resting places of these sometimes flawed but always faithful men and women, there is an overwhelming sense that we are truly surrounded by a great cloud of witnesses. The challenge is the same now as then: to run with perseverance the race that God has marked out for our generation in the same way as they did in theirs.

At the top of the hill, there is a white-painted wooden tower called the *Altarn*, which many people refer to as the prayer tower. The first structure here was actually built in the 1790s, nearly 50 years after the prayer watch first began. The current tower was erected about a decade ago as a public viewing platform, so it can hardly claim any direct historical connection with continuous prayer. However, the location is laden with heritage. It was here that Zinzendorf so frequently came to pray and seek God, here that the Herrnhut community held their open-air worship services, festivals and prayer vigils.

On entering the tower, the first thing that strikes us is the graffiti. Largely confined to a panel that seems to have been reluctantly surrendered for the purpose, people have scribbled prayers, Bible verses and entire psalms on the wall. For those who are able to accept felt-tip color rather than stained glass, it is clear that this is a place of pilgrimage. Climbing the spiral staircase, we emerge onto the broad circular balcony at the top.

Contrary to most of our contemporary theology, prayer can seep into the very fabric of a place. At the top of the Hutberg is a distinct sense of divine presence. Justin describes it as a richness in the spiritual atmosphere, a kind of depth that makes prayer flow strong and free. We pray for Germany, for the UK, for each other, and for the crazy current of 24-7 prayer in which we are all caught up. I honestly hadn't come expecting an emotional encounter or spiritual high, but in fact the power of God is tangibly here. Only our watches confirm that we have spent over an hour on the windswept tower.

When the Old Testament prophet Isaiah was given a vision of the glory of God (see Isa. 6), it led to a sense of renewal and commissioning. In more recent times, God took this insignificant village and made it another place of encounter and sending out. Today the question God asks is still the same: "Are you willing to come and meet with Me, and are you willing to go wherever I send you?"

CHAPTER 7

THEN SLAVE I SHALL BE

The only man who has the right to say that he is justified by grace
alone is the one who has left all to follow Christ.

DIETRICH BONHOEFFER

◆

I t was early on July 24, 1731, and Leonard Dober the potter was having a bad night. He lay awake in the dormitory
of the Single Brethren's house, his heart pounding, his
mind still full of images from a dream so vivid that it seemed more
than real. Even as his emotions began to settle, his mind raced
faster and faster with the implications of what he had just experienced. In his dream, Dober had witnessed images of the Negro
slaves in the Caribbean islands and had repeatedly heard the voice
of God calling him to go and preach freedom to the captives.

Dober's dream was most likely inspired by a talk given by
the count earlier that evening. Zinzendorf had just returned
from Copenhagen, where he had been on semi-official business
attending the coronation of King Christian VI of Denmark.
However, the tale he related to the single brothers was not one
of crown jewels or royal audiences, but instead concerned his
conversations with a slave named Antony Ulrich.

A Cry from the Wilderness

Antony came from the Danish-owned island of St. Thomas in
the Caribbean. He was a bright and confident speaker, but more

important, he had heard the message of Jesus Christ and was baptized as a believer. He had told Zinzendorf in detail about the situation of the slaves on St. Thomas, especially their spiritual condition. "If only some missionaries would come," he said, "they would certainly be heartily welcomed. Many an evening have I sat on the shore and sighed my soul toward Christian Europe; and I have a brother and sister in bondage who long to know the living God."[1]

Zinzendorf's personal commitment to the almost unknown idea of overseas mission dated back to the development of the Order of the Mustard Seed, and Antony made a powerful impression on him. He knew that the story would fall on similarly receptive ears at Herrnhut. Since their initial commitment to pray and prepare for missions work in 1728, a group of the Single Brethren had disciplined themselves to study the Bible, languages, geography and medicine, in the hope that these skills would equip them when the day arrived. The count had been active in encouraging and training this group. Now, for Leonard Dober at least, the wait appeared to be over.

Morning came, and with it the first doubts. Had he really heard from God, or was it just his own imagination? Having learned to look to the Bible for confirmation, he turned to the watchword for the day and was confronted with this verse: "For it is not a futile thing for you, because it is your life, and by this word you shall prolong your days in the land which you cross over the Jordan to possess" (Deut. 32:47, NKJV). With this apparent confirmation, Dober felt brave enough to take his friend Tobias Leupold into his confidence. As they walked together through the woods on the Hutberg that evening, Dober was astonished to discover that Leupold had felt the same call and had been waiting all day for an opportunity to share it with Dober! The two headed back to the village to join the evening hymn singing. When the two men, along with the singers, paused in the street outside Zinzendorf's home, they clearly heard the count turn to a guest and remark, "Amongst these brethren, there are messengers who will go to St. Thomas, Greenland, Lapland."

The next day, Dober and Leupold wrote a letter to Zinzendorf offering themselves to serve as missionaries to St. Thomas. Zinzendorf shared the circumstances (although not the names) with the rest of the congregation, and the community responded with cautious enthusiasm for the project.

The initial excitement was dampened, however, four days later by the arrival of Antony Ulrich himself. His appeal was as compelling as before, but he was also soberingly realistic about the conditions that any prospective missionary would face. He described the long hours, poor conditions and evening curfew under which the slaves labored. The only realistic way to live and work among them was to become a slave oneself. Many in the congregation concluded that the situation sounded impossible. Dober's sense of calling and conviction ran deeper. His response was simple and absolute: If the only way to reach the slaves was to share their condition, then a slave he would be.

Breaking Camp

In fact, it took a whole year before Dober's dream became reality. Part of the delay came down to the time it took to persuade the leaders of the Brethren that the mission was right, and part arose from Zinzendorf's desire that the young men should have plenty of opportunity to reflect and count the cost of what had every chance of being a one-way trip. Finally, in the summer of 1732, the congregation decided to settle the matter through prayer and the drawing of lots. They prayed that God would reveal His will, and Leonard Dober reached his hand into a box. He drew out a slip of paper at random. On it were written the words, "Let the lad go, for the Lord is with him."

The lot, however, did not yet approve the sending of Leupold, so Dober instead chose David Nitschmann the carpenter as his traveling companion.

On August 18, the two men were driven in Zinzendorf's carriage to Bautzen, and after they and the count had knelt to pray together by the roadside, they set out on foot toward Denmark. Their equipment consisted of the clothes they stood in, about 30 shillings in cash, the tools of their trades, and their traditional but deeply unfashionable three-cornered hats. Arriving at Copenhagen, they caused something of a sensation. The Danish West India Company was suspicious of their motives and refused to grant them passage on its vessels.

The court, however, was intrigued by these strange missionaries and rallied support for them. Acceptance from the court was due in part to careful ground-laying by Zinzendorf the year before. The Danish royal family had Pietist convictions, and Christian VI had secretly accepted membership of the Order of the Mustard Seed. It is not known for sure whether unofficial royal patronage was going on, but doors started to open for Dober and Nitschmann. They were given money by the chamberlain, encouragement by the queen, and medical equipment by the court physician. The royal cupbearer found them passage on a ship, and they arrived in St. Thomas on the thirteenth of December. The two men were among the first missionaries to be sent out in Protestant church history, the first to go as lay workers rather than theologically trained ministers, the first to be sent by a church rather than a state body or society, and the first to work among slaves.

Being refused the opportunity to sell themselves into slavery on the grounds that they were white, they took manual jobs on the plantations, which gave them close access to the slaves alongside whom they worked. They were not allowed to hold public meetings, so they met individually with the slaves in their homes. Initial progress was slow, and was hindered by the niggling opposition of the plantation owners and the often appalling witness of their so-called "Christianity."

David Nitschmann left four months into the trip as previously arranged, to report back to Herrnhut on the progress of this first missionary expedition. By the time he arrived, the second wave had already departed. Exploiting their favorable reception in Copenhagen and following on from the work of a state-sponsored Danish Halle missionary named Hans Egede, Matthew Stach, his cousin Christian and the irrepressible Christian David had already left to take the gospel to the Eskimo people of Greenland.

Dying to Tell

These first missionary expeditions were incredibly tough and showed no immediate signs of fruit in terms of people accepting Christ. In 1734, Tobias Leupold made the journey to St. Thomas to take over for his friend Leonard Dober and to extend their work to the neighboring island of St. Croix. He led a party of 18, which included both men and women. Within a year, 13 of them, including Leupold himself, were dead of yellow fever, malaria or dysentery. With no news coming back to Herrnhut, 11 more arrived in 1735. Two months later, 7 more were dead and still others had to return home due to their weakened condition.

In Greenland, things were no better. The cold and darkness were intense, food was short, scurvy was rife, and the language proved a massive barrier. The Eskimos made contact only to steal or beg. A smallpox epidemic hit the region. The Moravians stayed to nurse the sick but received little thanks for risking their lives. Sensing despair, Matthew Stach and two of his companions made a covenant to stick it out together, determining that they were there "not on the principle of sight but of faith."[2]

The same conviction affected the Herrnhut community. The prayer watch continued around the clock, constantly bringing the mission work before God in prayer. On congregation days, the whole community met to hear news and letters from the missionaries read out. Despite the sometimes chilling reports of sickness and opposition, they continued to volunteer for service themselves, year after year. During the decades that followed, Moravians went to the slaves of the Caribbean, the Eskimos of Greenland and Newfoundland, the black South Africans, and the American Indians. They reached Ceylon, South America, the Far East, and the Russian and Arab worlds. By the end of the century, this tiny village of around 300 people was responsible for sending out over 1,000 missionaries to virtually every part of the known world.

The environment in which these early missionaries found themselves was totally different from anything they had experienced in nominally Christian Europe. There were no precedents or instruction manuals that could tell them exactly how to convey the message of Jesus to peoples who had simply never heard of Him. Egede's approach in Greenland had been to try to teach a reasoned Christian theology, but his efforts had met with failure.

Zinzendorf's gut instinct, on the other hand, was to teach the love of God for individuals as shown to the world in the crucified Christ. The accuracy of his intuition was dramatically proven in 1738 when, back in Greenland, John Beck was talking with a group of Eskimos. The conversation followed the usual pattern: He tried to explain to them the basics of Christian doctrine, and they rapidly lost interest. Then, in a moment of inspiration, he read from a passage in Matthew's Gospel, which he had been painstakingly translating into their language. In slow and deliberate speech, he began to tell the story of the passion of Christ; how He had prayed in agony in the garden of Gethsemane, sweating drops of blood as He contemplated the death He was about to undergo. A young Eskimo named Kayar-nack, deeply touched by the words, came forward and demanded, "Tell me that again, for I, too, would be saved."[3] Where systematic theology had failed, the simple message of Christ crucified had broken through.

The same principle worked in the life of Wassampah, a violent and hard-drinking Mohican Indian who had been nicknamed "Tschoop" by Dutch traders in New York. His conversion became as notorious as his former life, and he went on to be a powerful witness among his own people. He summarized his experience as follows:

> Brothers, I have been a heathen, and have grown old among the heathen, therefore I know how the heathen think. Once a preacher came and began to explain to us that there was a god. We answered, "Do you think we are so ignorant as not to know that? Go back to the place you came from." Then again, another preacher came and began to teach us, and to say, you must not steal, or lie, or get drunk, etc. We answered, "You fool, do you think we don't know that? Learn first yourself, and then teach the people you belong to, to leave off these things, for who steal and lie, or who are more drunken than your own people?" And we dismissed him. After some time Brother Christian Henry Rauch came into my hut and sat down by me. He spoke to me nearly as follows: "I come to you in the name of the Lord of Heaven and Earth. He sends word that he is willing to make you happy, and to deliver you from the misery in which you now are. To this end He became a man, gave His life as a ransom for man, and shed His blood for him." When he had finished, he lay down on the floor, being tired from his journey, and fell into a

sound sleep. I then thought, what kind of a man is this? There he lies and sleeps. I might kill him, and throw him into the woods, and who would even know it? But this gives him no concern. However, I could not forget his words. Even while I slept I dreamed of that blood which Christ had shed for us. This was something different from what I had ever heard before. And I interpreted Christian Henry's words to the other Indians.[4]

General in the Field

Zinzendorf's involvement was not restricted to sharing his theories on how to preach the gospel. He was, rather, at the center of the entire missionary operation, interviewing the volunteers, providing resources and instructions, and maintaining correspondence. In December 1738, stung by critics who implied that he was happy to send his followers overseas to their deaths but unwilling to go himself, he resolved to visit St. Thomas to find out what had happened to the ominously silent mission there.

Zinzendorf was usually a poor traveler, but with characteristic faith he prayed and recorded the remarkable outcome as follows: "Since I had so much to do, I talked with the Savior, saying that it would not be convenient for me to be sick, and so I became well even before we sailed."[5]

Three missionaries, including a husband and wife team, accompanied Zinzendorf. As they approached St. Thomas, he was clearly nervous and, thinking aloud, asked, "What if we find no one there? What if the missionaries are all dead?"

"In that case, we are here," replied George Weber.

"*Gens aeterna* [the eternal people], these Moravians!" exclaimed Zinzendorf.[6]

The exchange summed up well the go-for-it attitude of the Herrnhut missions.

On their arrival, not a trace of the missionaries could be found. Some brief enquiries among the slaves soon provided the reason: far from being a failure, the mission had triggered a spiritual awakening among the Negro population, and over 600 had come to faith in Christ. Jealous at the baptism of these new believers and alarmed that the Moravians were teaching the slaves to read and write, the official Dutch pastor had managed to get them imprisoned on trumped-up charges. The Moravians had been in prison for three months, but far from impeding the work, their imprisonment had acted as a powerful testimony to the sincerity of their faith. The slaves gathered outside the prison window every evening to join the "St. Thomas Three" in impromptu hymn singing, which annoyed the plantation owners even more.

This was one situation that Count Nikolaus Ludwig von Zinzendorf was equipped to deal with. In a letter home to his wife, he reported, "I burst into the Castle like thunder." The governor was apparently scared out of his wits by the arrival of this high-ranking and extremely irate nobleman, and the missionaries were released within 24 hours. Having gained the initiative, Zinzendorf then worked hard to establish a more friendly relationship with the colonial powers. He also spent several weeks preaching among the slaves and putting into place enough organization for the mission to continue to grow.

Zinzendorf never excelled as a missionary in the field. He lacked the patience and cultural insight for dealing with native peoples. Practical deficiencies like his unwillingness as a young man at university to take his riding lessons seriously would eventually tell on him. However, as a motivator, leader and organizer, he is probably unequalled in history.

His spiritual insight and ability to learn from both successes and failures (including his own) were remarkable, and he used the skills he did possess wisely. He wrote detailed instructions for missionaries, in an age when there were no books or training colleges to refer to. His instructions were simple, incisive and seem relevant even today. The experiences and practical methods of the Moravians were to become part of the foundations for virtually all the great missionary movements of the nineteenth century.

By the end of Zinzendorf's life, 226 missionaries had gone out to previously unreached peoples around the world. This number *exceeded the total number of missionaries sent out by the entire Protestant movement in the whole of its previous history!* What is more, these missionaries were mostly ordinary, working-class people, without formal education or financial resources, and few of them were ordained clergy. Nowhere else was Zinzendorf's mustard seed principle more clearly at work. The tiny seed not only grew to global proportions during his own lifetime, but through its enormous influence as an inspiration and model, it truly "filled the whole earth" in the decades that followed.

Valley of Grace

Perhaps the best illustration of the effect that a single seed can have is the story of the Moravian missions to South Africa. The Dutch colonists and their official state church considered the native South African peoples to be subhuman and incapable of receiving salvation. Into this hell of bigotry and brutality came 26-year-old George Schmidt.

Schmidt had already spent six years in prison as a teenager for attempting to encourage believers in Austria, had watched his mentor Melchior Nitschmann die in his arms, and then had overcome the hurdle of learning the Dutch language and passing an examination in theological orthodoxy. Compared to these barriers, the scorn of the farmers and clergy hardly fazed him. He arrived in 1737 and set up Africa's first mission station in the quiet valley of Baviaanskloof ("Valley of Baboons") east of Cape Town.

Schmidt built a house and planted a pear tree in the garden. He made contact with the local Khoi, a semi-nomadic people who were already displaced and under severe pressure from farmers and settlers. He formed a school and taught the Khoi to read and write. He showed them how to farm and grow the food they needed to survive. In everything he gave quiet witness to the love of the crucified Christ. Five years later, the first native believer was baptized in the Steenbrans river.

The clergy were outraged. Schmidt's success in bringing prosperity, education and faith to the native people struck at the heart of their twisted theology. They manufactured a confrontation by raising technical questions surrounding Schmidt's ordination and then used their influence to have him expelled from the country in 1744. It was 50 years before the Moravians were allowed to return to South Africa.

On arriving back at Baviaanskloof in 1792, the three new missionaries soon located the ruin of the original house. In the garden, to their amazement, stood a giant pear tree—the result of the tiny shoot that Schmidt had planted. But even greater surprises were in store.

They soon made the acquaintance of an old woman named Magdalena. When she found out who they were, she introduced herself as one of the original believers who had been baptized 50 years previously. The light of faith still burned in her heart, and for half a century this remarkable woman had nurtured and led the indigenous church that Schmidt had founded. She drew out a small leather bag and asked if her daughter could read something from the New Testament. They listened astonished as this second-generation native believer read to them from a Bible given by Schmidt five decades earlier.

Within 10 years, the governor of the region was so impressed by progress at the settlement that he changed its name to Genadendal, which means "Valley of Grace." It grew to a community of over 1,500 people who were self-sufficient in agriculture and cottage industries, with a literate population and a strong spiritual life. In 1838, the first teacher training college in Africa was founded there.[7]

Genadendal flourished throughout the nineteenth century, in spite of jealousy and opposition from the settlers. It was not until the apartheid era that its downfall came: Its status as a "colored" community meant that the college was closed and the people were forced into menial jobs on the land.

In 1995, in recognition of its remarkable history, Nelson Mandela changed the name of the president of South Africa's official residence in Cape Town from "Westbrooke" to "Genadendal." When he made the announcement, he expressed one of the most remarkable public tributes to the selfless faith and vision of the Herrnhut missionaries—a desire that the office of president should also be and remain "under God's grace."

Berthelsdorf
Thursday, June 3, 2004, 18:00 local time

From the top of the *Altarn*, the village of Berthelsdorf is clearly visible less than a mile away down the hill. Finding it in the car proves to be slightly difficult, because someone has decided to dig up the road that connects the two villages, necessitating a complete closure. A prolonged detour finally brings us into the village from the other end. It was here that Zinzendorf's dreams of establishing a Christian community first took shape, and here in 1721 that he had a manor house erected for himself and his new wife, Erdmuth Dorothea. It is the manor house that we are now attempting to find.

Eventually, we discover that the missing road is the one that actually runs past Zinzendorf's former front door, but we are able to park a short distance away. Markus tells us to expect the place to be in a pretty sorry state. It was allowed to fall into disrepair during the Communist era, and as recently as 2000, questions over exactly who owned it were making attempts at repair impossible. However, all that now appears to be changing.

Outside the courtyard, a large sign announces that the place is under restoration with money provided by the Saxon government, a heritage trust and the national lottery. Inside, the main house is almost invisible under a straitjacket of scaffolding. A newish-looking office stands next to the entrance, but at six o'clock on a Thursday evening there doesn't actually seem to be anyone around. Ducking under the red-and-white tape used to cordon off the site, we walk cautiously into Zinzendorf's backyard.

The courtyard itself is a scruffy construction site. The remains of a small but elegant formal garden are barely visible. On three sides it is surrounded by a variety of buildings that must once have been stables, barns and workshops. The main door of the house itself is very much closed, but the date (1721) is clearly visible above the porch. There is still no one around, and we get the distinct impression that we are either a couple of years too early or 50 years too late.

The windows of the house must have been beyond recovery, because whatever remained of them has been removed by the restoration team. The openings are now either boarded up or braced with steel bars, presumably to add strength until they are confident of the main structure. Justin has managed to find one on the ground floor that still offers a decent-sized aperture. We gather round and peer in. The room is empty apart from some small piles of rubble and has the remains of an elegantly vaulted ceiling.

Without any discussion, but accurately reflecting all our unspoken thoughts, Justin swings himself up onto the sill and slides down into the building. Rather less elegantly, I squeeze my lanky six-foot-five frame through the gap and follow suit. There is no light inside, but open windows and roof sections provide enough daylight for us to see that we are close to the entrance hall. Inside, a sturdy-looking collection of beams and braces gives us confidence that the workers have stabilized the structure sufficiently and it isn't going to collapse around us. In the main hall, a temporary wooden staircase leads up to the next floor.

We wander randomly for a while through the maze of spacious rooms. Everything movable has been stripped out, but here and there part of a plastered ceiling or wall remains, offering an impression of how the place must once have looked. On the top floor, the ceilings are largely gone, but a new red-tiled roof is mostly on, giving a sense of purposeful progress in the restoration work.

Descending back down the wooden staircase and with our eyes now more accustomed to the gloom of the lower level, it is clear that the floor still consists of the original flagstones. Around the door they are worn smooth and concave by the passage of thousands of feet over a period of nearly 300 years. As always, it is this small feature that offers a sense of connection. How many times must the Zinzendorfs, de Wattevilles and others have walked across these stones? What messages of joy and grief, success and disappointment, have been delivered on this threshold?

Often when we pray, we find ourselves asking for something from God—our own hopes and desires phrased in our own words. As the three of us pray together in Zinzendorf's still largely derelict home, the words that come seem to originate from beyond our own ideas. The Old Testament prophet Amos wrote:

In that day I will restore David's fallen tent.
I will repair its broken places, restore its ruins,
and build it as it used to be (Amos 9:11).

Something inside us responds to this, and we begin to pray that God will restore Zinzendorf's fallen house. Physically, we can see it happening around us with these ruins of brick and stone. Spiritually, our cry is that the deeper heart of this place, the heart for persistent prayer, radical mission and authentic community, would also be restored in Herrnhut, in Germany, in the whole world and, yes, even in us.

CHAPTER 8

On the Road and Off the Rails

How is it that no one ever makes a mistake on purpose
but mistakes get made all the time?

Edward de Bono

The young university tutor Augustus Gottlieb Spangenberg would one day be internationally famous and
would take part in shaping the destiny of nations.
Although 23-year-old Augustus was blissfully unaware of it,
tonight that destiny hung in the balance. He was normally a
regular member of the Pietist meetings at Jena University, but
on this particular evening there was no big-name speaker
scheduled, and he had paperwork to finish. In the end he decided that he would make the effort to attend and, turning up
slightly late, he settled himself at the back of the hall.

At the front were two quaintly dressed visitors from a village named Herrnhut. As Andrew Beyer and Gottlieb Wried
stood up to speak, it was immediately clear that the students
were not in for another evening of academic theological debate.
With simple words but great passion and authority, the two
men began to unfold their story of changed lives, a trans-
formed community, and a visitation of God's Holy Spirit.
Spangenberg was deeply affected. In his diary, he wrote con-
cerning a later meeting, "I was present and kept silent, but my
heart rejoiced."[1]

The impact on Spangenberg and a number of the students at Jena was profound. Their meetings took on a new life and significance. They also felt a renewed compulsion to show the love of Christ in practical ways to the people around them. As a result, they established a number of free schools for poorer children in the suburbs of Jena. Spangenberg was heavily involved, and Zinzendorf encouraged them in the work. In 1730, Spangenberg visited Herrnhut and was again deeply impacted by what he found there. He accepted a post as superintendent of the orphanage at Halle, but the magnetic draw of Herrnhut proved too strong. In 1733, he returned for good, committed to serving God in whatever ways he could be of use. He went on to become the dynamic leader of the Moravian missions to America and one of the key figures in the growing movement.

Revival Hits the Road

What happened at Jena was soon repeated in towns and villages across Germany and the whole of Europe. Within weeks of the "Moravian Pentecost" of August 1727, messengers had started to leave Herrnhut carrying their remarkable stories of personal and corporate transformation. Their purpose was to stir up others to start living the same life of prayer, faith and fellowship that they had found. They were not seeking to make converts, but instead encouraged those they met to live wholeheartedly for Christ within the structures and authority of their own church background. They would thus encourage Lutherans to remain a part of the Lutheran Church, but also to gather together in small groups to pray, worship, share fellowship and support one another. The emphasis was on warmth, simplicity and genuineness. Divisive theological debate was firmly discouraged, in favor of the practical application of faith to the realities of daily life.

The movement to reach out had started without a plan, a name, a budget or any kind of organized objective other than spreading the love and message of Jesus. It was not until many years later that the groups were officially given a name: the "Diaspora," or "scattered ones."[2]

The rate of growth among these societies was phenomenal. By 1748, 540 communities outside the Baltic provinces were reported as being in connection with the Moravian movement. In the Baltic area, 45,000 people were attached to Diaspora societies.[3] Groups were founded in Britain, Ireland, Holland, Sweden, Denmark and even as far afield as Russia. In spite of this, the Moravians obstinately resisted the growth of their own "denomination." The majority of Diaspora members did not follow Spangenberg in joining the communities at Herrnhut or elsewhere. When new converts wanted to make an expression of commitment, they were directed to the established church of their own nation or region. Even congregations or societies led by Moravian ministers were not considered permanently Moravian in affiliation. They were only under their care until they could be handed over to the recognized local church.

To understand this remarkable refusal to develop an organized movement out of a groundswell of popular renewal, we have to get inside the mind of Zinzendorf and grasp something of his beliefs regarding the nature of church.

A Religion of the Heart

Zinzendorf consciously rejected the shallow and politicized concept of church in eighteenth-century Europe. He instead looked for a heart religion: a deep, personal and intimate knowledge of Jesus Christ as Savior and Friend. It was this personal relationship with Christ that made a person a Christian, not any external declaration of affiliation or observance of religious rituals.

The true church of Jesus Christ, according to Zinzendorf, was therefore an invisible body of believers, scattered among the visible denominations. This was the diaspora he recognized: not a geographical scattering, but the fact that those sharing the "heart religion" could be found scattered within every Christian tradition. His experience showed that he could share genuine fellowship with Catholics, Protestants, Lutherans, Anglicans and many others, wherever he found those who shared this same inward personal faith in Christ.

Zinzendorf believed that the greatest offence against the church was nominalism. He knew only too well that many so-called Christians were involved for purely social and political reasons, or had a "faith" that was based only on intellectual assent and included no element of personal experience. The former would bow to anything that fashion or authorities dictated. The latter were caught up in endless arguments over doctrine, which promoted division and stagnation rather than a dynamic unity. The Diaspora societies were one way of bringing together the true believers, those who knew the "heart religion," and lifting them out of the mass of compromise and division without starting yet another sect. They were an expression of the church within a church idea that had so influenced Zinzendorf's Pietist upbringing.

Suspicious Minds

The best way to keep a secret is not normally to send people out to spread the news over half a continent. Zinzendorf had already become a well-known and rather controversial figure in Dresden, and the activities on his Berthelsdorf-Herrnhut estates were steadily attracting opposition from several quarters.

Zinzendorf's family was still upset and embarrassed at his neglect of official duties to concentrate on religious matters, and would have been quite happy to see the downfall of what they considered to be his pet project. The church and state authorities were perpetually suspicious of anything that looked like a new sect or movement, regardless of its professed orthodoxy and loyalty. Local clergy and landowners were losing their parishioners to the growing community. Even the Pietists at Halle were becoming cool toward the count. They resented their lack of direct influence at Herrnhut and Zinzendorf's rejection of their strict and systematic doctrine of the process of salvation, which denied that anything good existed in the human spirit prior to conversion.[4] Zinzendorf himself had outlined the growing divide with his statement, "The essence of Christianity does not consist in being pious but in being joyous."[5]

Matters came to a head in January 1732, when a group of commissioners representing the king and kingdom of Saxony arrived from Dresden. They announced that they had come to examine the community for theological orthodoxy. They attended the various Sunday services and interviewed numbers of the Brethren privately. After a tense wait of over a year, the verdict was finally announced. The Schwenkfelders, a small Protestant sect who had been living as part of the community since its founding, were identified as dissenters against the Lutheran Church and were ordered to leave Saxony. The Moravian Brethren were granted an edict of toleration and allowed to stay as long as they behaved themselves quietly.

Although the Brethren had been given a reprieve, the situation was still alarming to Zinzendorf. To be merely tolerated as a sect seemed ominous, and the wording "behaving themselves quietly" sounded distinctly like a threat. Thus, Zinzendorf took steps to safeguard them in the event that the worst should happen. On paper at least, the Herrnhut congregation could be divided into two groups: the traditionally Lutheran Germans and the Moravians. Zinzendorf now negotiated to send a party of Moravians to establish a settlement in the new American colony of Georgia.

Their purpose was twofold: They had a strong desire to work as missionaries amongst the American Indians, but they were also there as an advance guard in case a place of refuge was required for the whole community. On a personal front, the count decided to take the increasingly inevitable step and have himself ordained as a Lutheran minister. To do so in Saxony in its current climate would have been politically difficult, not least for the bishop who performed the ceremony; but the more neutral southern German faculty of Tübingen proved willing. Zinzendorf passed an examination in Lutheran theology and was accepted into the ministry in December 1735.

The response to any future threat was now in place. The Moravians could leave and enjoy complete freedom of religion in America. The Lutheran part of the congregation would remain at Herrnhut, with Zinzendorf himself as their legally recognized pastor. However, what happened next caught the count completely off guard.

The Pilgrim Congregation

Zinzendorf was never someone to be provoked by attacks on his character or activities. His difficult childhood had taught him tough but valuable lessons about coping with bullies. In reflective moments he was more concerned with how Christ viewed him than with the opinions of his social contemporaries. Throughout life, his policy was to avoid being drawn into public arguments by leaving personal criticism unanswered, unless it clearly threatened the wider movement. What he should have recognized was that he himself was under greater threat than the Brethren he was trying to protect.

In 1736, an alliance of Zinzendorf's political enemies managed to convince the new king, Augustus III, that the count's activities should no longer be tolerated. Zinzendorf, at the time, was on the way back from Holland, where he had been involved in negotiations to start the South African mission and the planting of a new community on the Herrnhut model at Heerendyk. Arriving at Cassel, Zinzendorf was met by one of the David Nitschmanns, who was holding in his hands a royal edict that banished the count from Saxony on the grounds that he had encouraged heresy. At the same time, he heard news that a second royal commission was going back to investigate Herrnhut.

It turned out that the Moravians had little to fear from the authorities. At the end of his stay at Herrnhut, Dr. Löscher (one of the commissioners) burst into tears and announced, "Your doctrine is as pure as ours, but we do not possess your discipline."[6] The official report recommended that the Moravians should be allowed to stay, noting that their industrious community was already making significant contributions in taxes to the royal coffers. As for himself, Zinzendorf took the banishment in his stride. His initial response to Nitschmann was:

> It matters little. I could not have returned to Herrnhut anyway for ten years, for the time has come to gather the pilgrim congregation and preach the Saviour to the whole world. Our home will be that particular place where at the moment our Saviour has the most for us to do.[7]

While Zinzendorf clearly had enemies in high places, he also had no shortage of friends and admirers. One of these invited him to visit Marienborn in central north Germany as a possible base for his operations. While there, the count's attention focused on the adjacent castle of Ronneburg. The building itself did not have a great deal to commend it: It was crumbling, rat infested and partly open to the elements. Christian David cast a professional eye over it and announced that conditions had been better back in Greenland. However, Zinzendorf was convinced. To him, the poor surroundings were actually a selling point. The area was host to around 60 homeless families, whom Zinzendorf saw as in special need of the love of Christ. Soon, the Ronneburg became the new temporary headquarters of the Moravian movement.

Whatever their social class or background, every member shared the same food, lifestyle and initially rather basic accommodation. The poor inhabitants of the area, who presumably expected to be moved on, were instead offered food and friendship. The children frequently ate with Zinzendorf's own young family. A school was started to teach them to read and write. Within a few years, a new community named Herrnhaag ("The Lord's Grove") had grown up based on the Herrnhut model and was the center of the most dynamic and organized missionary operation on the globe. It housed schools for 600 children and a training college for ministry and mission (established by Spangenberg), which attracted candidates from all over Germany.

Although Herrnhaag became the operational headquarters, the "pilgrim congregation" was frequently on the move. The count and his associates spent time at locations in Germany and England. From 1741 to 1743, Zinzendorf traveled to Pennsylvania, where his ideas for the future role of the Moravian movement in church affairs began to take shape.

A Congregation of God in the Spirit

Pennsylvania in the 1740s was a mess of arguing factions composed of the dozens of strong-minded groups who had gone there to start a new life. A popular term of abuse for a completely godless person was to say that he "professed the Pennsylvania religion."[8] Few of the groups had any significant impact in caring for the spiritual or practical needs of the communities they were supposed to serve. Zinzendorf saw the distressed situation as an accurate portrait in miniature of the churches in the world at large.

Deploying his gift for leadership and his charismatic personality, he managed to bring together the various groups to a series of meetings known as the "Pennsylvania Synods." At these gatherings, he began to expound the set of ideas that came to be known as the "Tropus concept."

The starting point was the "heart religion" that Zinzendorf regarded as the essential character of any authentic Christian faith. He was convinced that, even among the odd sects who had made their home in Pennsylvania, there could be found believers who shared the heart religion and were thus capable of forming a bond of unity based on their common experience of Christ.

Zinzendorf viewed each of the various denominations within Christianity as a tropus, or "training camp," there to train the believer in the essentials of faith. As such, the existence of different groupings was not in itself a bad thing. In fact, each tropus could bring a unique contribution to the church as a whole. One might have a rich tradition of liturgy, another a distinctive gift in worship, another a passion for prayer or mission, and others the ability to relate to a specific cultural group. However, Zinzendorf saw that somehow the different groups needed to come together as a functioning whole. The basis of unity would not be complete agreement on doctrine or expressions of faith, because these formed a God-given diversity. Rather, it would be a shared knowledge and experience of Christ as Savior and Friend. The concept was neatly summed

up in a phrase that was to become not only the motto of the
Moravian church but also a popular motto among Lutherans,
Calvinists, English Puritans, Quakers and, later, Roman
Catholics: "In essentials, unity; in non-essentials, liberty; in all
things, love."[9]

According to Zinzendorf, the mission of the Moravian
movement was twofold. First, it was a tropus in its own right—
a revival of the old Bohemian Brethren, with a rich heritage of
practical faith and discipline to contribute. Second, the
Moravian movement's flexibility in doctrine and historically
good relationships with several branches of Christianity prepared it to become a vessel for the elusive "whole" in which all
tropuses could unite. What Zinzendorf proposed in light of
these insights was absolutely breathtaking. He intended
Pennsylvania to be a pioneer and model for the unification of
the entire Protestant stream of Christianity, and ultimately the
entire church of Christ in the world.

Zinzendorf's name for this joining of all the denominations or tropuses into a single body, retaining their diverse
character but held together by a common bond of unity in
Christ, was the "Congregation of God in the Spirit." He offered
the *Unitas Fratum* ("Unity of Brethren"), the extended community of believers that had arisen out of the Herrnhut revival, as
the vessel in which this Congregation could initially be formed.

The settlers who had come from Herrnhut and its daughter communities were identified as belonging to three different
tropuses: the Lutheran, the Reformed and the Moravian.
Zinzendorf was the de facto leader over all three tropuses,
though he presented himself as a Lutheran pastor (and even
went so far as to resign his office as a Moravian bishop to clarify the point). Thus, under Zinzendorf's leadership, the
Lutheran, Reformed and Moravian tropuses were quite clearly
already living and working together as a single body, the Unity

of Brethren. In the Pennsylvania Synods, Zinzendorf was inviting the other groups to join them in forming a united Congregation of God in the Spirit.

The concept was brilliant. Visionary. Inspired. It appeared to offer a workable solution to over 1,000 years of harmful division within the Church. Unfortunately, the timing was wrong. The Pennsylvania sects were still experiencing their first taste of freedom in America and were unwilling to compromise it by joining any kind of Moravian-led federation. Also, the idea was so radical, so far ahead of its time, that most (including many of the Moravians themselves) simply could not get their minds around it. Despite leaving America having achieved a basic willingness among the groups to meet and talk together, and having incidentally spurred many of them to get on with their own pastoral work, Zinzendorf also left with the goal of genuine unity still frustratingly out of reach.

The Sifting Time

The journey back to Europe in January 1743 was perhaps a foreshadowing of what was to come. As Zinzendorf's ship approached the southwestern tip of Britain, it was lashed by storms so severe that even the experienced Captain Garrison feared for his life. When Zinzendorf heard of this, he calmly told the captain that the storm would be over in two hours. As the ship was driven nearer and nearer to the rocks, Garrison came below decks and prepared himself for the end. After the two hours were up, Zinzendorf requested that the captain go up on deck to check the weather. The captain recorded the astonishing outcome in his log: "Scarcely had I been there two minutes, when the storm subsided, the wind changed to the southwest, and we were soon out of all danger."[10] Zinzendorf later confided in him that God had clearly spoken to him as he prayed about the peril they were in, which was how he had been able to predict the outcome with such accuracy.

Arriving back in Germany, Zinzendorf did not find the situation entirely to his liking. Prussia and Silesia had a new ruler, whose view of life was completely unspiritual and shrewdly pragmatic. He had no interest whatsoever in who or what the Moravians worshiped, but he did recognize that they were industrious settlers with a gift for turning rundown areas into thriving economic centers. As such, he granted them complete freedom of conscience and invited them to come and plant more communities on the Herrnhut model in his own territories. To the Brethren this had seemed like a good opportunity to extend their work. To Zinzendorf it smelled of compromise with an atheistic authority.

Inexplicably, Zinzendorf's response to the generosity and tolerance of the atheistic ruler was to reject all worldly wisdom and demand a simpler, childlike expression of faith in Christ. This might have started as a useful insight, but it very rapidly became a fanatical obsession. Child*like*ness degenerated into child*ish*ness. The Order of the Mustard Seed took a back seat, in place of a new "Order of the Little Fools."[11] Jesus Christ, the Lamb of God, became "our dear little lamby." Zinzendorf's leadership role was that of "papa,"[12] and so on. The count similarly set aside his brilliant intellect and broad experience as valueless, and insisted instead on the drawing of lots as the only valid method of determining the will of God.

After the abandonment of good sense, the next thing to go was good taste. The theological emphasis on the "blood and wounds" of the crucified Christ as the heart of the gospel became a grotesque wallowing in the physical details of the nail prints and side wound. The experience of being spiritually "born again" was described using explicit sexual metaphors. The dangers of sexual temptation were "warned against" using similarly graphic and culturally unacceptable language. Combined with the enthusiasm for childishness, the results were bizarre and disturbing. Believers were encouraged to visualize themselves as little worms, bathing in the blood of Christ, among other things.

These expressions appeared in Zinzendorf's sermons, in the life of the communities, in pamphlets and other literature, and especially in the prolific songwriting of the Brethren. Additions were made regularly to the Moravian hymnbooks during this period, but the new material published as the *12th Appendix* in 1748 demonstrated the depths to which they had sunk.

The outside perception of the Moravians at this time is illustrated by the kind of interest they started to attract. In London, characters such as William Blake and Emanuel Swedenborg were briefly associated with the Moravian society in Fetter Lane. Both authors were known for their interest in sexual mystery religion, and it is easy to see how the Moravians' use of overt sexual imagery would have drawn them in. Neither developed close connections, but the association has been a target for critics and conspiracy theorists ever since.

At the center of the movement, Herrnhaag was both the worst offender and the means of spreading these ideas to other Moravian settlements. Herrnhut, with a generation of stability behind it and under the watchful eye of the Saxon authorities, was the least affected. Zinzendorf had never been short of enemies, and now a virtually unlimited source of ammunition for their attacks was flowing off the Brethren's own printing presses. Having initiated and encouraged the whole situation, Zinzendorf had also failed to rein in its worst excesses by basing his "pilgrim congregation" in London, away from the center of the action. Although he had been warned by many trusted friends of what was resulting from his ideas, he had dismissed them as unspiritual. Now several things came to a head at once.

In Pennsylvania, where new arrivals from Herrnhaag were bringing the infection, Spangenberg found the situation unsustainable and resigned his leadership of the community. In London, Zinzendorf was joined by a former soldier from Herrnhut named Karl von Peistel, who seemed to succeed where others had failed and forced the count to recognize exactly how bad things had become. Finally, a new heir to the estates around Herrnhaag took control and decided to deal firmly with his settlers-turned-fanatics. He issued a decree demanding that they must either cut off all connections with Zinzendorf's movement or leave the territory within three years.

When Zinzendorf finally acted, he was as forceful as ever. He stood up before the entire leadership and publicly repented of his own actions, declaring: "Ah! my beloved Brethren, I am guilty! I am the cause of all these troubles!"[13] He publicly withdrew the various items of offensive literature that had been produced. The noxious *12th Appendix* was consigned to the dustbin. Zinzendorf called Spangenberg back from America to apply his immense practical talents and wisdom to sorting out the mess.

As for Herrnhaag, the community did the one thing their landlord had assumed could never happen. They left. Abandoning an investment worth many millions in modern currency, a permanent population of over 600 left their lavish and extravagant base and redistributed themselves to other locations around the globe. Many went to America. Some moved to other Moravian settlements. Still others reevaluated their lives and sensed a renewed call to the Diaspora work or the mission field. Most went in 1750, and within the allotted three years, all had gone. Herrnhaag was never resettled.

The seven-year period from 1743 to 1750, which became known as the "sifting time," was a sad landmark in the history of a remarkable movement. In some ways the excesses came close to destroying all that had been achieved. Yet while it was degenerating into pathetic self-indulgence in its spiritual expression, Herrnhaag still remained the vital center of the greatest missionary movement on the planet. Individuals who were one day speaking and acting in a way that made impartial observers cringe, the next day up and went, giving their lives sacrificially to powerfully effective works on the edges of the known world.

In spite of the lasting damage it caused, this period was remarkable in at least one respect: It exemplified the lesson of both the Bible and history—that even godly movements can and do sometimes fall into heresy and fanaticism. However, the "sifting time" ended with the result that the Moravians were left with increased maturity, more robust systems of self-regulation, and a newfound humanization of their elevated leadership. In this respect they became a living parable of the gospel of grace and redemption that they had always preached. The simple vow to remain true to Christ again proved itself a reliable compass in the stormiest of circumstances.

Zinzendorf's own reputation never fully recovered after 1750. His enemies now possessed an ample store of accusations that, although dealt with, could be proven in black and white to have occurred. The need to deal constantly with often wild and unfounded criticism remained a drain on his time and energy. The aftermath of the period also drove a wedge between the Moravians and a man who was already becoming one of the most influential figures in the English-speaking world: John Wesley.

Dresden International Airport
Friday, June 4, 2004, 07:30 GMT

After a welcome opportunity to stop off and meet Markus's wife, Andrea (who is away working at a youth camp outside Dresden), and a late-night kebab-eating session in the Neustadt, we wake up tired again on Friday morning. This is the aspect of pilgrimage that I have never fully understood. You experience the emotional high of arriving at what you thought was the destination, and then realize that you are actually only halfway through the journey.

A little later than planned, we arrive at the airport and say our good-byes to Markus. He hands over an extensive collection of presents for Pete Greig (apparently it's some kind of tradition between the two of them), which includes twelve litre-bottles of beer and a ghastly Zinzendorf T-shirt that was rather embarrassingly on sale in the Moravian bookshop in Herrnhut. I do a quick recalculation to ensure that the beer bottles aren't going to adversely affect our center of gravity, and Justin and I are given a short ride back out to the plane.

The weather in Dresden is beautiful: clear blue skies and every indication that it is going to be a lovely day. Unfortunately, the forecasts are unanimous in confirming that a warm front is crawling toward us across central Germany. In its wake it is dragging a belt of low cloud, mist and drizzle that looks completely impenetrable. This could seriously hold things up. Lacking better options, we decide to give it a go and weave our way through the maze of taxiways and holding points to Dresden's main runway.

The first hundred miles or so pass easily. We fly high, making the most of the endless visibility. The conversation today is subdued, the prayer less exploratory and more focused. We have touched something of God while we have been here, and it is going to take time to fully digest our experiences. Leipzig-Halle calls us with a rather pointed request to confirm our altitude, and I discover that I have busted their airspace by 300 feet. Okay, hint taken! Can't afford to get too relaxed.

South of the Harz Mountains, we meet the advance guard of the approaching weather front. Above us the blue sky has been replaced by a lowering gray overcast, and ahead the crystal-clear air is turning hazy and indistinct. Berlin Information confirms that the weather at Paderborn is 2,500 meters visibility with light rain and a 600-foot cloud base. There's no point in pushing on into that, much better to land now while we still have decent conditions and try to come up with a new plan.

Our nearest diversion airfield is Nordhausen, which we locate easily enough; but their radio frequency is silent and the signals square is displaying a "special precautions" symbol. There is no reason why we shouldn't land, but the idea of a deserted aerodrome with no meteorological information or (equally important) coffee doesn't appeal. The next best option looks like the jaw-breakingly named Obermehler-Schotheim, about 10 minutes' flying to the south. I dial up their frequency and silently rehearse the name a couple of times in my head to avoid making a complete hash of pronouncing it.

Obermehler-Schotheim responds promptly, and its ample runway looms into view through the deepening haze after a brief GPS-assisted search. From the air this is one very strange airfield. Almost brand new, with a huge concrete apron marked into dozens of neatly spaced parking bays, but not a single aircraft anywhere in sight. On landing we discover the reason why: It was built by the Russians just before the fall of the Berlin Wall, but never completed. A smart prefabricated control tower looking rather lonely amidst the acres of concrete marks the local municipality's modest attempt to make a go of things since then.

One thing that Obermehler-Schotheim does have (apart from two friendly enough staff and a half-decent coffee machine) is a superb Internet weather terminal. In full-color animation, it tells us the depressing story. The weather front will be here within the hour, bringing with it low cloud, mist and rain. We seem to have little choice but to sit here and wait for it to pass overhead, which at current rates of progress will be at least seven hours away.

Whatever spiritual lesson we were expecting from today, the art of waiting wasn't on our agenda. There is absolutely nothing to do. The lounge is comfortable enough, but the nearest town is a taxi ride away and has no features that promise to make it worth the fare. We sit for hours. Telling our respective life stories in a bit more detail than we have previously managed consumes the first hour. Justin reads a book. I write some thoughts on the journey so far in my journal. Waiting is only stressful if you are consumed by thoughts of what you could or should have been doing with the time. For brief moments I manage to acknowledge that an enforced interlude of reflection might not be a bad thing. Then the nagging pressure to get home, to meet the demands and expectations of our respective lives and schedules, imposes itself and I look impatiently back out the window at the sky.

The weather moves agonizingly slowly from dull to wet to damp to misty then back to overcast again. I wait too long to put the cover on Alpha Mike and get unnecessarily wet rushing out to do it as the first rain starts to fall. I become an expert on the tiniest details of every ridge of hills surrounding the airfield. As the features vanish then reemerge through the mist, it becomes clear that the cloud is at last starting to lift. The computer says that Paderborn still has low cloud and rain, but Hanover to the northwest is clearing up nicely. From there, conditions are good all the way through to the Dutch coast.

At last a sense of purpose fills the scene. We take the cover back off Alpha Mike and taxi the short distance to the pumps to refuel. Another airplane emerges from a hangar on the far side of the field and heads off on a local flight. We climb up to the control tower to say our thanks and good-byes and to file a flight plan. It is now too late to get back to England tonight, but it seems feasible to make it to Ostend on the Belgian coast. From there it will be only a quick hop across the Channel in the morning and we will be home.

CHAPTER 9

'TWAS ON THE GOOD SHIP SIMMONDS

So fine an old man I never saw! The happiness of his mind beamed forth in his countenance. Every look showed how fully he enjoyed "the gay remembrance of a life well spent."

ALEXANDER KNOX, OF JOHN WESLEY

Around noon on Sunday, the small sailing ship was hit by the third Atlantic storm in a week. The wind and waves rose steadily, and as the winter darkness closed in, the diarist again considered the possibility that he might not survive another night. The ship carried just over 100 passengers, most of whom were crouched nervously in the space between decks. The wooden hull did nothing to dampen the howling wind or the relentless pounding of the sea, and a tense atmosphere of fear was building in the cramped cabin.

Although preoccupied with the weather, the diarist was a methodical man. At 7:00 P.M., as had become his custom, he made his way to join the party of 26 Germans who normally celebrated a service of worship at this time on a Sunday evening. This group had increasingly impressed the diarist during the three months of the voyage from England to America. They were willing to carry out menial tasks that the English passengers considered beneath themselves, saying, "It is good for our proud hearts" and "Our loving Savior has done more for us." Some of the other passengers, interpreting this humility as weakness, had taken to pushing the Germans around or striking them roughly. In spite of this, the Germans never complained and made no attempts toward revenge. Reaching the group as their service was about to begin, the diarist's entry for January 25, 1736, recorded what happened next:

> In the midst of the psalm with which their service began, the sea broke over, split the mainsail in pieces, covered the ship, and poured in between the decks, as if the great deep had already swallowed us up. A terrible screaming began among the English. The Germans calmly sang on. I asked one of them afterward, "Were you not afraid?" He answered, "I thank God, no." I asked, "But were not your women and children afraid?" He replied, mildly, "No; our women and children are not afraid to die."[1]

The name of the ship was the *Simmonds*. On board was Governor James Oglethorpe with 100 settlers bound for the recently founded colony of Georgia. The "Germans" were the second party of Moravians from Herrnhut, sent to boost their presence in the colony. The diarist who recorded the events of that night was a 32-year-old English clergyman named John Wesley.

A Crucial Connection

John Wesley went on to become one of the best-known and most controversial figures in British history. In a recent BBC poll, Wesley's name comfortably made it onto a list of the 100 greatest Britons of all time, and it is likely that his name will still be there in the Ws long after transitory celebrities such as entertainer Robbie Williams (also featured) have been forgotten.

However, in 1736, he bore only a partial resemblance to the passionate revivalist he later became. In his mind he understood and accepted the truth of Christ as well as anyone. In his will, he was fully determined to serve God; at Oxford University he and his friends had formed a religious society strikingly similar to those Zinzendorf founded at Halle. Wesley's zeal had earned his group the nickname "the Holy Club" or "Methodists." Despite these achievements, a conflict lay in Wesley's heart: Deep down, he was honest enough to admit that he did not possess the assurance of God's love and an utter confidence in salvation, which the Moravians had so clearly displayed during the storm.

Two weeks after Wesley's encounter with the Germans, the *Simmonds* landed in Georgia. The following day, Wesley went to Spangenberg, the leader of the Moravian community, and asked his advice on how he should conduct himself in the task that lay ahead of him in reaching the Indians with the gospel. Spangenberg's profoundly insightful answer touched right to the core of Wesley's dilemma, as his journal entry shows:

> "My brother, I must first ask you one or two questions. Have you the witness within yourself? Does the Spirit of God bear witness with your spirit that you are a child of God?"
>
> I was surprised, and knew not what to answer. He observed it, and asked, "Do you know Jesus Christ?"
>
> I paused and said, "I know He is the Saviour of the world."
>
> "True," replied he; "but do you know He has saved *you?*"
>
> I answered, "I hope He has died to save me."
>
> He only added, "Do you know yourself?"
>
> I said, "I do." But I fear they were vain words.[2]

The quiet witness of the Herrnhut families on the *Simmonds* and the words of Spangenberg in Georgia started a chain reaction deep inside the spirit of John Wesley. Fueled by the Spirit of God, this reaction grew over the next few years until it exploded with nation-shaking consequences. At the time, though, Spangenberg and Wesley had practical matters to concern them. They had the welfare of their respective communities to consider, and both shared a desire to reach out to the Indian nations who lived in the region around the Savannah River.

Cowboys and Indians

In order to achieve their objectives, both men had to deal with the charismatic General Oglethorpe. Oglethorpe was the founding visionary behind the Georgia colony, and his vision was a grand one. He was a dedicated Christian philanthropist and wanted to provide a place of refuge for debtors (who were then frequently imprisoned), former convicts and victims of persecution to start a new life. Parliament looked on his scheme favorably for a more pragmatic reason: The location of the colony provided a useful military buffer against the Spanish presence farther south. Whatever the motives, a charter was granted and the first colonists arrived in 1733. Oglethorpe had strong views on the lifestyle and morals his colonists should adopt, and soon added further regulations banning slavery and rum in Georgia.

Oglethorpe was a larger-than-life character in many respects. One local historian has described him as "an eighteenth-century mixture of Mother Teresa and John Wayne."[3] He took a keen interest in the colonists' welfare, putting his authority and his own money on the line to ensure that the poor were adequately cared for. One pastor recognized in him "a man having great reverence for God and his holy Word and Ordinance; a cordial love for the servants and children of God; and who desired to see the name of Christ glorified in all places."[4] On the other hand, his strong views and brash style made for him many enemies. He was a bachelor until late in life and was accused of frequenting brothels. It was also held that he was involved in starting the Savannah lodge of Freemasons.[5]

In 1737, Oglethorpe traveled to London, where Zinzendorf was then staying. Although seemingly very different characters, the two immediately struck up a favorable relationship. Both were idealists, energetic organizers and men of action determined to put their ideas into practice. It was probably on this occasion that Oglethorpe accepted membership of the Order of the Mustard Seed. That he was willing to sign such a demanding and Christ-centered "oath of allegiance" casts an encouraging light on his alleged Masonic involvement. Most Christians are rightly alarmed by the darker spiritual aspects of Freemasonry, but it is important to retain an attitude of faith and grace toward those in its grip. By 1737, Oglethorpe was evidently willing to decide in favor of a radical and clearly stated commitment to serve Jesus Christ above all.

One of Oglethorpe's earliest contacts was Tomochichi, leader of the Creek nation of American Indians. Oglethorpe showed him considerable respect, entering into a treaty with him to gain his blessing on the new settlement, and brought him to England to meet the king. In spite of previous encounters with Spanish conquistadors whose preferred method of "conversion" was at gunpoint, Tomochichi continued to think deeply about God and His dealings with mankind. On first meeting the newly arrived Wesley, he stated (through an interpreter):

> I am glad you have come. When I was in England, I desired that some would speak the great Word to me and my nation then desired to hear it; but now we are all in confusion. Yet I am glad you have come. I will go

up and speak to the wise men of our nation; and I hope
they will hear. But we would not be made Christians as
the Spaniards make Christians: we would be taught,
before we are baptized.[6]

Wesley was to be frustrated in his hopes to reach the Indians
with the gospel. He was repeatedly refused permission to spend
time amongst them, on the basis that "Savannah must not be left
without a minister." Spangenberg and the Moravians fared slightly better. They developed close relationships with Tomochichi,
and Zinzendorf wrote a remarkable letter to the chief. It reads
almost like one of Paul's letters in the Bible. He starts:

> Wise man! Dear King Tomo Chichi!
> I have heard that you are searching for wisdom. The
> wisdom you are looking for, you in fact already possess;
> because this is wisdom: to know what you don't know.[7]

Zinzendorf goes on to outline concisely the entire gospel
message, from the condition of all humanity before God, to
God's initiative in sending Jesus to die in our place and the necessity of a personal response. He ends the letter:

> I write because I love you, and because my brothers and
> sisters love you and have written to me concerning you.

> Your slave Zinzendorf.

The final greeting really does mean "slave," rather than the
more conventional ending "your servant." For a European
noble to address an Indian leader in this way was radical in the
extreme, but to Zinzendorf it was a natural extension of the way
he viewed the world. He was a slave to Christ first and foremost,

therefore a slave to the gospel message, and thus a slave of everyone to whom that message was sent. Tomochichi did eventually find the faith for which he had been searching, and he too became a member of the Order of the Mustard Seed.

Strangely Warmed

Wesley stayed in Georgia for a little under two years. He arrived with dreams of preaching the gospel to the native people; he left broken and disillusioned. His ministry had been hampered by his being drawn into the petty rivalries and disputes of the colony. In particular, he had badly mishandled his relationship with Sophy Hopkey, the daughter of an influential merchant. The two were initially attracted, but Wesley procrastinated for so long that she gave up and married someone else. Wesley then later refused her Holy Communion over a minor matter, and the whole affair blew up in his face. Accusations flew, writs were issued and, realizing that the situation was becoming impossible, Wesley returned to England in 1737. His inner turmoil continued, and writing in his diary on the return trip he reflected, "I went to America, to convert the Indians; but oh! who shall convert me?"[8]

The answer to this question came sooner than he expected. Five days before Wesley's ship landed in England, a newly ordained Moravian minister named Peter Böhler had arrived from Germany on his way through to Carolina. Wesley was introduced to Böhler and helped him find lodgings in London. Wesley then introduced Böhler to James Hutton, a London bookseller who was fast becoming a crucial link in the chain. He knew the Wesleys and the Oxford Methodists, and had formed a society in Aldersgate Street with some of them. He had also come into contact with the Moravians and had recently been introduced to Zinzendorf, who was staying in Chelsea.

John Wesley and Peter Böhler met regularly over the next three months. Wesley was confused but fascinated by the idea of "the holiness and happiness" that, according to Böhler, were "the fruits of living faith." Wesley had strived most of his life to be holy and was virtually resigned that such a pursuit of God neither could nor should make him happy. Böhler claimed that both could be given in an instant, as a direct gift of God. Yet Wesley felt himself "clearly convinced of unbelief, of the want of that faith by which we alone are saved." He asked Peter Böhler whether, in the light of this, he should give up preaching. Böhler's reply was inspired: "Preach faith till you have it; and then, because you have it, you will preach faith."[9]

The next day, Wesley visited a condemned man in prison and preached to him the possibility of complete forgiveness and peace if he would put his faith in Christ. He preached to others with such passion and conviction that he was barred from the pulpit of several churches in London for stirring things up. In spite of this, he still acknowledged that he did not yet know this faith for himself. He looked to the Bible and the doctrines of the Church of England, and found everything that Böhler was telling him in theory. Yet he questioned whether an instant, transforming conversion could really happen in practice, even after being introduced to numbers of individuals who claimed this experience for themselves.

At the beginning of May, Peter Böhler was due to leave England for Carolina. In a letter to Wesley from Southampton, he wrote, "Beware of the sin of unbelief, and if you have not conquered it yet, see that you conquer it this very day, through the blood of Jesus Christ."[10]

On May 24, 1738, John Wesley woke up early and read in his Bible the words, "You are not far from the kingdom of God" (Mark 12:34). In the afternoon he was invited to a service at St. Paul's Cathedral in London, and the choir sang the words, "Out of the deep I have called unto Thee, O Lord: Lord, hear my voice." The two insights seemed to reflect Wesley's own hope and desperation. In the evening he went "very unwillingly" to the society at Aldersgate Street. Someone was reading from Luther's introduction to the biblical letter of Romans. In Wesley's own words:

> About a quarter to nine, while he was describing the change which God works in the heart through faith in Christ, I felt my heart strangely warmed. I felt I did trust in Christ, Christ alone, for salvation; and an assurance was given me that He had taken away my sins, even mine, and saved me from the law of sin and death.[11]

John Wesley, always the master of dry understatement, had experienced the touch of God's love and grace at last. Within a year, the spark that had "strangely warmed" Wesley's heart would begin to set the length and breadth of Britain ablaze with the wildfires of spiritual revival. His first instinct was to seek out those who could best direct him on the next stage of his journey. Two weeks later he set out for Germany, determined to visit the Moravian community at Herrnhut.

Separated at Birth

Wesley was by no means going to be an uncritical observer of what he found. His dry humor and razor-sharp wit later earned him the uncharacteristic praise of the great critic Dr. Samuel Johnson: "Sir, you talk well on any subject!" Even while traveling through Germany, his journal records his scathing impression of Cologne as "the ugliest, dirtiest city I ever yet saw with my eyes."

On reaching Herrnhut, any skepticism that Wesley might have been harboring was melted away by what he found.

He observed a life of deep faith and practical deeds that seemed to match that of the biblical followers of Jesus. Of the people, he noted:

> [H]ere I continually met with what I sought for, viz., living proofs of the power of faith: Persons saved from inward as well as outward sin, by "the love of God shed abroad in their hearts"; and from all doubt and fear, by the abiding witness of "the Holy Ghost given unto them."

Wesley (the Oxford academic) listened to Christian David (the carpenter) preach, and was so impressed that he wrote out virtually the entire text of the sermon. He also met with many others of the Moravian leaders. The disciplined lifestyle of the community appealed to Wesley's own "Methodist" ideas, and their infectious joy and peace were compellingly attractive. As the time came for him to leave, in his journal he longingly wrote:

> I would gladly have spent my life here; but my Master calling me to labour in another part of his vineyard, I was constrained to take my leave of this happy place. . . . O when shall THIS Christianity cover the earth, as the "waters cover the sea"?[12]

Wesley's first impressions of Zinzendorf were not so favorable. Their personalities clashed from the outset. As the Moravian historian Hutton observed, "If a poet and a botanist talk about roses they are hardly likely to understand each other."[13] Zinzendorf, by nature, was a poet, an idealist and a dreamer, while Wesley's intellect was ruthlessly practical. Both possessed leadership gifts of such extreme magnitude that any movement would have struggled to handle more than one of them at a time. On returning to England, Wesley discovered that the meetings that Peter Böhler had started in James Hutton's house on Fetter Lane had developed into a full-blown society. Böhler had left detailed instructions on how to run things, including a division into "classes" and "bands" for Bible study, fellowship, confession and prayer. This arrangement was typical for Moravian Diaspora societies and was to become one of the distinctive features of early Methodism. The Fetter Lane Society became the first port of call for Moravians traveling through London. On New Year's Eve 1738, they held a "watch night" service at which John and Charles Wesley, George Whitefield, Hutton, Ingham and other leaders of the Moravians and Methodists in Britain were present. "About three in the morning," wrote John Wesley, "as we were continuing instant in prayer, the power of God came mightily upon us, insomuch that many cried out for exceeding joy, and many fell to the ground."

Three months later, Wesley received an urgent invitation from George Whitefield to come and assist him in preaching to the crowds who were coming to listen to the gospel at Bristol in the west of England. In spite of his discomfort at the idea of preaching anywhere other than in a church, Wesley went. On the first Sunday, he spoke to more than 7,000 people in the course of three open-air meetings. With that, the riot of preaching, repentance, deliverance, civil disruption and community transformation that marked the "Great Awakening" in Britain had begun.

With Wesley frequently away traveling, divisions began to appear in the Fetter Lane Society. On his return, Wesley was invariably drawn into the conflicts of personalities and ideas but was able on several occasions to sort things out. While he was away, the Moravians had no leader of similar caliber to restrain the kind of theological division that they normally sought to avoid. Instead, a recent but strongly opinionated young convert named Philip Molther appeared on the scene and soon had the place split into outright factions.[14] Wesley and Molther publicly disagreed, and in 1740, following a bitter debate, John Wesley left Fetter Lane for good.

Zinzendorf was in London in 1741 and attempted reconciliation, but the two men found each other's views as irritatingly incomprehensible as ever. From that point onward, the Moravians and Methodists in Britain increasingly went their separate ways.

Brothers at Arms

The problems at Fetter Lane were rapidly resolved by Molther's departure and the arrival in 1741 of Spangenberg, whose unassuming genius and gift for clearing up other people's messes soon had the place back in thriving order. Fetter Lane was registered as a Moravian congregation, although in typical style many of the English members also retained membership of the Anglican Church. Led by James Hutton, they established the "Society for the Furtherance of the Gospel," which became the main means for funding mission work in the British colonies. They also supported a number of evangelists, including men such as John Cennick, who had initially worked alongside Wesley and whose work in Ireland was, for a time, similarly thriving.

In spite of their similar mission and methods, Wesley remained a strong critic of the Moravians. Just as the Methodist movement was entering its most dramatic phase of initial growth, the Moravians went through their period of "sifting time" excesses. This only confirmed in Wesley's mind that they were unstable and untrustworthy, and he published a number of pamphlets in which he was sharply critical of them. It was not until late in life that his enduring respect for James Hutton enabled a measure of reconciliation. Even Wesley and Zinzendorf were eventually able to "agree to disagree," though they never really worked together.

Contrary to Wesley's feelings, in the early stages of the Great Awakening in Britain, many commentators felt that the Moravians would become the driving force. In fact, it was Methodism that had a more visible impact on British society. Methodist congregations were established across the length and breadth of the country. The social changes that accompanied this revival of faith, especially in the poorer segments of society, were immense. Drinking dens, which sowed violence and poverty at the heart of working communities, were closed down, not because of the authorities but for a simple lack of trade. Pit ponies that dragged wagons of coal in the mining villages of industrial England could no longer understand their drivers, who had ceased to curse and swear at them! Writing after the French Revolution, historian Elie Halevy advanced the theory that Methodism was significantly responsible for preventing Britain from undergoing a similarly violent transition from monarchy to republic.[15]

The Moravians did not ultimately play a larger role for a number of complex reasons. For example, although they planted large settlements on the Herrnhut model at Fulneck (near Leeds in Yorkshire), Ockbrook (near Derby) and Bedford, which aimed to serve many congregations that had come under Moravian care as a result of revival preaching, they never intended these smaller groups to become a part of the Moravian church. They only took on responsibility for congregations by invitation and always made it clear that these worshipers were ultimately to be returned to the care of the Church of England, whom they regarded as the "legitimate" national church. Once a month, the Moravian workers led their congregations to the nearest parish to celebrate Holy Communion, and they took pains to cultivate good relationships with the local priest.

The result was a calculated and successful attempt to do the work of God without encouraging the growth of the Moravian denomination. On the one hand, this was an admirable stance given the long history of harmful division within the Church. However, the Moravians may have idealized the possibility that their work would succeed in reviving and renewing the established Church. In fact, eighteenth-century England probably bore more resemblance to one of their unreached overseas mission fields than to the "Christian country" they perceived it to be. It took a movement such as Methodism, which was unafraid of pioneering new methods of mission and expressions of church on home territory, to really reach the people with the message and love of God. In several cases it was the Methodists, not the Church of England, who ultimately took over responsibility for Moravian congregations.[16]

The same principle was at work wherever the Moravians were found. They showed hardly a trace of sectarianism. In strict numerical size, they started and remained small. In terms of effectiveness and influence, they proved to be one of the most potent and pioneering movements of their age, and in this respect their legacy is still felt even today.

OBERMEHLER–SCHOTHEIM AIRFIELD, GERMANY
FRIDAY, JUNE 4, 2004, 17:30 GMT

Lifting off into the dull gray skies, Alpha Mike touches cloud base at an encouraging 2,000 feet. The highest point on our planned route is a radio mast on a hilltop at 1,756 feet, but there is no rule saying we have to fly right over it, and it soon slips past to our left.

Alpha Mike skims across tree-lined ridges and soars out over valleys dotted with picture-postcard villages. The flying, however, is intense. High ground and low cloud are an uncomfortable combination. Thankfully the wind is calm, which means that we have less to fear from invisible currents swirling around the hills; but at the back of my mind I am very aware of the need, always, to have a Plan B. Right now, Plan B would involve making a sharp U-turn and retracing our steps to Obermehler-Schotheim. Not an attractive prospect, but a safe one because it takes us back through known territory and clear weather.

A patch of blue sky is briefly visible through the clouds, and a shaft of evening sunlight falls onto the valley ahead. The moment lifts our spirits, and they are lifted further by the arrival of checkpoint 1—the neat grass airfield at Bad Gandersheim. We have been airborne for half an hour, but it feels like much longer. Turning west on our new heading, the hills are lower but the haze is starting to return. This wasn't supposed to happen; the forecast says it should have cleared by now. Ahead, the next ridge is barely visible, the tops shrouded in mist and lowering cloud.

Time for Plan B. I execute a tight 180-degree turn and consider the options. Low cloud lingering on the hills is hardly an unusual occurrence. To the north, a broad valley leads down into the low-lying plains and clear weather near Hanover. The navigation is simple: just follow the river and the railway line, and we're there.

The valley feels comfortable—a mile wide and plenty of space to maneuver. Something is definitely wrong with the weather, though. It seems to be coming down all around us. Visibility is still reducing, and the cloud base is falling as fast as the ground is descending, so we're not gaining any height at all.

There is an old aviation saying, normally told in clubhouses on days when the weather is too poor to fly, that observes, "It is much better to be Down Here wishing you were Up There, than Up There wishing you were Down Here." Right now, I am definitely wishing that we were Down There. According to the map, we should be nearing the town of Hameln, and it emerges from the haze right on cue. The hospital has a large helipad surrounded by grass, and for a brief moment it looks tempting. No, let's be serious here. There is still Plan C, one that every pilot is trained for—it's just that I am loath to use it. There are plenty of broad, flat meadows down by the river. Any one of them should be big enough to make what the textbooks dryly refer to as a "precautionary landing." Of course, if the ground is too soft or the field too short or the pilot not skillful enough, the aircraft may be damaged or unable to take off again, but at least the crew should walk away unscathed.

According to the map, the next town is called Rinteln, and it has a small airfield—a proper one, with a 600-meter tarmac runway and everything. If we can just keep going for a few more minutes, this has to be a better option than trying our luck with a field. I attempt to raise them on the radio, but there is no answer. We push on down the valley. Visibility is getting worse by the minute, and a few drops of light rain spatter the Perspex in front of us. The map says the airfield is on the near side of town. The GPS says it's two miles ahead at one o'clock.

All we can see is a new industrial estate. *God, we've come this far; please let us find this airfield* . . .

"There it is!"

Sure enough, there is the runway, about a mile ahead to the right of our nose. I have never been so happy to see a short stretch of tarmac in my entire life. I lower the flaps to stabilize our approach speed and rattle through the landing checks. Sixty-six knots, height looks good, everything has to be just right, we're coming in on a short, wet runway with not much margin for error, full flap as we approach the boundary hedge, power off, flare, stall warner sounds . . . and we're down. With all that adrenaline flowing, the landing is near perfect, and Alpha Mike slithers to a halt in not much more than half the distance available.

I turn the airplane around and taxi back toward the deserted hangars and control tower. My fingers run mechanically through the shutdown checks, and the propeller jerks to a standstill. All is quiet in the cockpit apart from the slowly decaying whine of the instrument gyros. We pull off our headsets and I slump back in the seat until the effect of mental exhaustion and endorphin rush manage to cancel each other out.

Fortunately I succeed in getting hold of Dresden airport on my mobile phone, and they are able to cancel our flight plan. Having landed at the wrong airfield, if we don't let someone know where we are, there could be search-and-rescue helicopters out anywhere between here and Belgium. As we take out our luggage and get the cover on Alpha Mike, a car draws up by the gate and a young man gets out.

The driver turns out to be Andreas, a member of the flying club who happens to be back from Bremen for the weekend. He has noticed the unfamiliar British-registered aircraft and stopped by to check it out. Immediately thoughts of "good Samaritan" spring to mind. Not only does he speak excellent

English, but he also offers to call around and find us a hotel room for the night, then insists on driving us up there himself. By the time we arrive, the hotel has finished serving food, but the owner takes pity on us and rustles up a meat salad and a couple of very welcome lagers. They have a wedding party on, but there are still two rooms available. The party is loud but seems good-natured (lots of oompah music and lederhosen—leather shorts—in evidence). The rooms are clean and have soft beds and warm showers. We fall asleep, grateful for the kindness of others, and with a promise from Andreas that he will arrange for us to be picked up if we give him a call in the morning.

CHAPTER 10

TO THE ENDS OF
THE EARTH

Call me whenever you desire, wherever you desire,
however you desire. . . . Only may your good spirit guide me and
lead me through the snares of the world as on level ground.

JAN AMOS COMENIUS

The young Baptist minister was not easily discouraged. He had been born and raised in poverty in rural England, and even now at the age of 30 he still had to ply his trade as a shoemaker in order to support his family while he pursued his spiritual vocation. For a number of years he had held the conviction that taking the gospel out to every branch of humanity was a fundamental aspect of Christian calling. On the wall of his workshop, he kept a crude leather map of the world that he had made himself, and as he worked he would pray for nations who had never heard the good news of Jesus Christ.

His fellow leaders were by no means convinced that the sending out of missionaries was necessary or even appropriate. When he first introduced the idea at one of their meetings, he was told, "Young man, sit down. When God pleases to convert the heathen, He will do it without your aid or mine."

One of the minister's sources of information and inspiration was the snappily titled magazine *Periodical Accounts Relating*

to the Missions of the Church of the United Brethren. In its pages he
had read details of the mission work supported by James
Hutton's society, and of the English Moravians who had already
gone out to do exactly what he was now proposing. Nearly a year
later, he took several of these magazines to a meeting at a house
in the English Midlands town of Kettering. During the discussion, he threw the magazines down on the table and with them
the challenge, "See what the Moravians have done! Can we not
follow their example, and in obedience to our heavenly Master
go out into the world and preach the Gospel to the heathen?"[1]

The result of that meeting was the formation of the Baptist
Missionary Society. The young minister—William Carey—is
widely known today as "the father and founder of modern missions." Within two years he left for India, where he was to spend
the remaining 41 years of his life working among the Bengali
people around Serampore.

Passing on the Torch

William Carey was born in 1761, 30 years after Leonard Dober
first felt the call to leave Herrnhut for the island of St. Thomas.
Just one year before Carey's birth, Nikolaus Ludwig von
Zinzendorf had died in Herrnhut at the age of 60.

Zinzendorf had been humbled by his responsibility for the
troubled "sifting time," and afterward was never entirely free of
the need to defend the movement against the criticisms that it
had fueled. He was also forced to lay aside his personal disinter-
est in financial matters and to recognize that his own estates
were mortgaged to the hilt. It was not that the projects had
been financially disastrous; the settlement communities were
powerful centers of wealth creation. It was simply that the work
had expanded so fast on so many fronts that the demands for
cash were always one step ahead. There had also been several

costly cases of poor judgment and administration. Zinzendorf's final decade was devoted partly to these issues, but
mainly to his first love: pastoral work and encouraging fellowship. He traveled extensively among the 20-plus settlements
that had been planted on the same model as Herrnhut, and also
among the Diaspora societies and congregations. However, his
base remained at Herrnhut, where he was the pastoral heart of
the community.

Countess Erdmuth Dorothea died in 1756. Zinzendorf was
deeply affected by the loss and also by a sense of guilt that he
had so often left her to shoulder incredible responsibilities
alone and had taken her remarkable talents and devotion for
granted. A year later he remarried, to Anna Nitschmann, the
woman whose election to leadership at the age of 15 he had initially opposed. She had long since become a trusted coworker
and the formidable leader of the Single Sisters for over 25 years.
Though married, they carried on separately with their respective work. By 1760, both were showing signs of illness, and on
the eighth of May, Zinzendorf was clearly close to death. To his
old friend David Nitschmann, he said:

> Did you suppose, in the beginning, that the Savior
> would do as much as we now really see, in the various
> Moravian settlements, amongst the children of God of
> other denominations, and amongst the heathen? I only
> asked him for a few first-fruits of the latter, but there
> are now many thousands of them.[2]

Nikolaus Ludwig von Zinzendorf went to be with the
Savior he loved and trusted so deeply on the ninth of May,
1760. His school-friend and fellow Mustard Seed initiate
Frederick de Watteville was by his side. Anna Nitschmann was
already too ill to keep watch with her husband, and she passed

away just 13 days later. They were buried in the Zinzendorf family plot at the center of God's Acre on the Hutberg. The inscription on Zinzendorf's gravestone is still clearly legible, and the last line translates, "He was chosen to bear fruit; fruit that would remain."

Fruit has two important characteristics. It is a valuable crop in its own right, and it also contains within it the seed to reproduce itself. The pioneering missions movement that so inspired William Carey is just one example of how Zinzendorf's mustard seed of faith grew to bear fruit in both of these respects.

Fruit That Remains

Zinzendorf had always struggled with a paradox in his ambitions for the Moravian movement. On the one hand, he felt a clear sense of calling to facilitate the rebirth of the Brethren Church. On the other, he had no desire to create another denomination and was much more interested in expanding the Unity of Brethren to somehow encompass all believers everywhere.

It was a strange church that had come into being by Zinzendorf's death in 1760. Across Europe, its remarkable settlement communities had only a few thousand members, but many tens of thousands more had come to faith through their work and strongly identified with the Moravians through their Diaspora societies and congregations. In the Caribbean, the Moravian church was composed almost entirely of black slaves, led and inspired by missionaries who still worked sacrificially without any support from larger and better-resourced denominations. In England the Moravian church had achieved legal recognition, was on friendly terms with the established church, and had statutory rights to extend their work overseas. Throughout the world were scattered mission stations and outposts, many at the center of growing congregations of indigenous believers.

In North America, the focus had moved to Pennsylvania where, under the leadership of Spangenberg, two more dynamic communities had been founded at Bethlehem and Nazareth. They pushed the concept of communal living and working to its ultimate expression. Every member voluntarily submitted to work in the settlement's "Economy," and from the revenue that was generated, the community supported a continuous presence of workers in mission fields across America. Their motto expresses their zeal: "Together we pray, together we labor, together we suffer, together we rejoice." "In our Economy," said Spangenberg, "the spiritual and physical are as closely united as a man's body and soul; and each has a marked effect upon the other."[3]

Zinzendorf himself had believed that within 50 years, the work of the Moravian movement would be completed. In fact, the momentum that he had created proved unstoppable. The Moravian church gradually transitioned to become a more conventionally structured Christian denomination. Their numbers remained small, due mainly to the selfless determination of the early pioneers to extend the kingdom of God rather than their own influence. This fact in itself stands as a challenge to our size-obsessed, personality-driven, empire-building culture—a culture to which the Church is by no means immune. Of Moravians today, around half live in the Caribbean, reflecting the pioneering work of Leonard Dober and the others who followed him. Their relative strength in the United States is due in no small part to the early leadership of Spangenberg. The seemingly random Moravian presence elsewhere around the globe shows the breadth of vision of the Moravian missions movement.

Fruit That Reproduces

William Carey was neither the first nor the last person to be inspired by the Moravian missionaries. When the London

Missionary Society was founded, they turned to the Moravians
for advice. In response to 11 specific questions, La Trobe (the
British secretary for Moravian missions) provided them with
a comprehensive explanation of their approach and methods.
In Germany, the Leipzig and Basel societies owed their origins
to Moravian influence.[4] For every missionary society founded
with the direct involvement of the Moravians, hundreds of
volunteers for mission work were personally challenged and
influenced by the example of the Herrnhut pioneers.

Even more surprising was the role played by the Moravians
in the campaign for the abolition of slavery in the British
Empire. Zinzendorf himself had willingly lived and worked
among the slaves as moral equals, but he had no desire to challenge the social order and in fact considered political reform a
poor substitute for the "true freedom" of all believers in Christ.
However, in the very act of bringing dignity, education and faith
to the slaves among whom they worked, the Moravians had
unwittingly driven a vital nail into the coffin of slavery itself.

When William Wilberforce launched his famous campaign
for the abolition of slavery in the British parliament, one of the
most powerful arguments deployed against him was the sug-
gestion that the slaves were savages, incapable of handling the
gift of freedom. His opponents asserted that they would either
collapse into barbarism or rise up in revolt the moment their
chains were removed. Wilberforce countered this argument
thanks to information he received from his friend La Trobe, the
Moravian missions leader. La Trobe provided Wiberforce with
a detailed account of the Moravian work among slaves in the
Caribbean. When he laid this evidence before parliament,
Wilberforce was able to prove that slaves could live peacefully
in faith and dignity when given the opportunity. Thus, the
Moravians made a valuable contribution to ending an injustice
without ever directly challenging it.

The influence of the Moravians on the start of the Great Awakening in Britain and America cannot be underestimated. It is unlikely that John Wesley would ever have become the fiery revivalist that he did if it were not for the influence of Peter Böhler and others. The Fetter Lane Society, started by Böhler on the Moravian model, was a formative influence on both the Wesleys and George Whitefield. The system of classes and bands, which was the lifeblood of early Methodism, had its direct origins in the lifestyle of the community at Herrnhut.

The Return of the Hidden Seed

One of the most remarkable sights in nature is said to be the response of a desert to heavy rain. Seeds that may have remained dormant for decades suddenly burst into flower in a riot of color and life that emerges apparently from nowhere.

When Comenius prophesied that the hidden seed of the near-extinct Bohemian Brethren would flower once again, he had caught hold of a spiritual principle whose fulfillment worked on an even larger scale than the renewal that occurred under Zinzendorf 100 years later. The seed of Comenius's day was sown by Jan Hus's vision. Hus had, in turn, been inspired by Wycliffe, whose reformation work and Bible translation faced intense opposition and whose followers were brutally suppressed.

Like a volcano whose periodic eruptions can be traced through history, there is something about simple, authentic faith in Jesus Christ that seems to defy the efforts of human institutions to suppress or corrupt it. This expression of true faith had a brief, explosive eruption of vision in the time of Wycliffe and Hus. It poured out a steady stream of fiery devotion during the years of the Bohemian Brethren. Then it lay dormant for 100 years through the seventeenth century, all the while with Comenius's prophetic time bomb ticking away deep inside it. It exploded into life once again with the Moravian renewal of 1727. It formed new volcanic islands through Methodism during the eighteenth and nineteenth centuries. Even as these began to cool, a new vent was opened with the "blood and fire" of William and Catherine Booth and the Salvation Army.

The volcanic hot spot marked by these eruptions of faith in Christ is significant because it has brought revival and hope throughout the history of Western culture. Now, at the beginning of the twenty-first century, if you type the word "Herrnhut" into an Internet search engine, there is evidence that the seismic tremors of an imminent eruption are discernable once again. Mixed among the history and heritage sites are reports from many nations of people being drawn back to Herrnhut. There are articles by respected teachers, dreams from prophetic visionaries, exploits of radical youth groups, and web-logs of nameless, faceless disciples. All seem to share a conviction that God wants to bring His church back to the DNA contained within the "hidden seed," which was once enlivened by the rains of heaven that fell on this otherwise insignificant village.

To respond truly to the promise of the hidden seed, the challenge of the mustard seed requires more than a commitment to recognize and build upon the past. For Zinzendorf, the "rich young ruler" who could have taken a life of comfortable privilege as a matter of birthright, the response began with a decision to lay down everything for the sake of Jesus Christ. Out of this resolve flowed the inevitable impulse to submit his life to the service of others and to the gospel message. The promise of the ring ("None of us lives for himself") sounds like an act of self-denial. In fact, it was an act of releasing that led to fulfillment and fruitfulness.

Jesus lived and died in a way that displayed the ultimate expression of this principle. His disciples in every age have heard His call to "follow me," and their stories testify to the promise that accompanies the challenge. Jesus said:

> Listen carefully: Unless a seed is buried in the ground, dead to the world, it is never any more than a seed. But if it is buried, it sprouts and reproduces itself many times over. In the same way, anyone who holds on to life just as it is destroys that life. But if you let it go, reckless in your love, you'll have it forever, real and eternal.[5]

Reckless love and a life that is both real and eternal: Surely these are fruit worth risking the seed of our lives in order to obtain.

Hills Above Rinteln, South of Hanover
Saturday, June 5, 2004, 09:30 local time

Andreas had advised us against making an early start, as low clouds in the valley would still be a distinct possibility until the sun came up. In fact, as we descend to the bar for breakfast, it is shaping up to be quite a pleasant morning. There seems to be one technical hitch: Justin's phone has a flat battery and mine is unable to raise Andreas on the number he has given us.

We needn't have worried. The Rinteln jungle telegraph has obviously been active, and before we can arrange for a taxi, a tall, powerfully built man walks into the bar. We approach him cautiously and ask if he is looking for the pilots from England. He confirms that he has come at Andreas's request to offer us a lift back down to the airfield. We shake hands and tell him our names. He says we can call him "Fritz."

Up close, Fritz seems a formidable character. His strong features are topped by a shock of steel gray hair. He looks very much like my first flying instructor, but if asked to guess at his former occupation, I would have him as the commander of a Heinkel squadron. He opens the boot of his car to stow our bags, and amongst the contents are a Lycoming aero-engine manual and a spiral-bound folder with a Luftwaffe emblem on the cover. *Hmmm.* I ask him what kind of aircraft he flies. "Oh, I fly pretty much anything" is his cryptic response.

Down at the airfield, things are coming to life. The weather forecast is good, and they are getting a couple of gliders out ready to start the day's activities. We fill the fuel tanks to the brim, and with a bit of help phone through our revised flight plan. We are a day behind schedule, and to recover lost time we decide to try for Goodwood on the south coast of England in a single hop.

We spend a while saying our good-byes at Rinteln. The people here have been very good to us, and we want them to know that their kindness is appreciated. Finally, we taxi carefully over the glider launch cables and line up for departure.

After all the problems of yesterday, the weather over western Germany is excellent. Visibility must be more than 30 miles in every direction, and I can easily see and avoid the occasional shower drifting majestically across the plains. By the time we reach Holland, the sun is high and the views are incredible. The inland seas are a sparkling blue, and soon the endless beaches of the French coast come into view. When we turn to cross the Channel at Calais, the white cliffs of Dover are already clearly visible. The sight is unexpectedly moving: How many sailors and airmen returning to English shores must have encountered this view as their first glimpse of home?

From Dover, the final leg takes us over the South Downs and on to the busy grass airfield at Goodwood. We try to sound as casual as possible when announcing ourselves as inbound on a flight plan from Rinteln in Germany. I'll bet that's a first for their control tower log! Just over four hours and 400 miles after taking off, we touch down, tired but extremely satisfied, on English soil once again.

Justin orders a taxi and I order fuel for the final hop back to Southend. Our good-byes seem extremely un-final. With or without the airplane, our respective journeys into the future (sometimes via the past) look set to continue together for a good while yet.

The last leg home coincidentally follows a route very similar to my original qualifying cross-country flight eight years ago. What then seemed like a great adventure, pushing back the boundaries of my own capabilities, is now a short positioning flight tagged on to the end of a 1,000-mile story. I have to drop Alpha Mike off on the far side of the airfield for a maintenance check, which leaves me nearly a mile to walk back to the car. In Rinteln this morning, people offered us their time and friendship when we needed it most. In Southend I stick my thumb out to save myself a walk, but no one stops.

Arriving back home, I am greeted by flags and bunting up the front of the house, drawings chalked on the doorstep, and an outrageous, extravagant welcome from Lisa and the girls. We drink Markus's beer and talk long into the night. I guess that pilgrims of old must have been welcomed back in similar grand fashion. Our modern lives can become enslaved to a routine of comfortable mediocrity that even the travel and extreme entertainment industries fail to penetrate. Maybe the antidote is to rediscover a rhythm of feast days and fast days, of journeying and homecoming. Tonight is a celebration in the Anderson house, and we are all the richer for it.

Some will undoubtedly ask what we think we have achieved. In some ways the journey stands by itself and has a meaning and purpose independent of any wider context. However, it seems uncoincidental that we were in Herrnhut while 24-7 prayer rooms are multiplying across the globe and many Christians are recognizing an imperative to reopen ancient wells of spirituality. The call to rebuild Zinzendorf's fallen house of prayer, unity, community and mission seems as relevant back in England as it felt real and urgent in the derelict manor house at Berthelsdorf. The Moravian story and heritage is a remarkable one that has impacted the destiny of this nation and the world before. God willing, it will do so again.

Zinzendorf would surely have smiled at the story of our journey. I suspect that his advice would be simple: Keep traveling together, keep telling the story and keep dreaming. It is in sharing our stories of Christ's love, as expressed through His life and death and the lives of His true followers, that the gospel is spread and disciples are formed. As Zinzendorf himself once said, "I recognize no Christianity without fellowship." If ever there was a time for a new "fellowship of the ring," it is surely now.

THE RENEWED ORDER OF
THE MUSTARD SEED

One of the many intriguing aspects of Zinzendorf's life that inspired me to write this book was the semisecret spiritual society he founded as a teenager and which subsequently shaped much of his life and work. The Order of the Mustard Seed offers a simple but incredibly challenging model for Christian discipleship that is still utterly relevant 300 years after its founding.

In *The Vision and the Vow*,[1] author Pete Greig makes a case for Christians in the twenty-first century to consider adopting a version of Zinzendorf's vow as their own "rule of life." In many ways, the Mustard Seed vow adds nothing to the essentials of the Christian faith. Its three elements (to be true to Christ, to be kind to all people, and to take the gospel to the nations) simply reflect the most fundamental commands Jesus gave to His followers (to love God with everything you've got, to love other people as much as you love yourself, and to go and make disciples of all nations).[2] However, many people are finding its clear focus on these essentials to be an invaluable compass in helping them to live as disciples of Jesus in a complex and confusing world. Its simplicity also makes it something that Christians from any background or tradition can identify with and share as a basis of fellowship and unity.

We are not attempting to reestablish the original Order of the Mustard Seed, and there is nothing that you can join as such. We are, however, encouraging individuals to consider establishing an expression of it with their friends as an aspect of their shared Christian commitment. If you have questions or are interested in finding out more, visit www.mustardseed order.com for information, articles, testimonies and practical resources.

ENDNOTES

Introduction

1. The story of 24-7 Prayer is told in Pete Greig and Dave Roberts, *Red Moon Rising* (Lake Mary, FL: Relevant Books, 2003). See also www.24-7prayer.com.
2. Pete Greig, *The Vision and the Vow* (Lake Mary, FL: Relevant Books, 2004).

Chapter 1: Little Lutz

1. A. J. Lewis, *Zinzendorf the Ecumenical Pioneer* (London: SCM Press, 1962), p. 21.
2. James E. Hutton, *A History of the Moravian Church* (London: Moravian Publication Office, 1909), sec. 2.1.
3. Ibid.
4. John R. Weinlick, *Count Zinzendorf* (Bethlehem, PA: Moravian Church in America, 1956), p. 23.
5. Hutton, *A History of the Moravian Church*, sec. 2.1.
6. Gerhard Reichel, *Der "Senfkornorden" Zinzendorfs*, trans. Markus Laegel (Leipzig, Germany: 1914).
7. Most of the inhabitants of Herrnhut originated from Moravia, in the eastern part of the modern-day Czech Republic.
8. For the full story, see Pete Greig and Dave Roberts, *Red Moon Rising* (Lake Mary, FL: Relevant Books, 2003) and www.24-7prayer.com.

Chapter 2: The Fellowship of the Ring

1. John R. Weinlick, *Count Zinzendorf* (Bethlehem, PA: Moravian Church in America, 1956), p. 36.
2. The idea of using Zinzendorf's vow as the basis for a contemporary "rule of life" is explored in Pete Greig, *The Vision and the Vow* (Lake Mary, FL: Relevant Books, 2004). To find out more, visit www.mustardseedorder.com.
3. This document is held in the Moravian archives in Herrnhut.
4. Herbert Spaugh, "A Short Introduction to the History, Customs and Practices of the Moravian Church," New Philadelphia Moravian Church, www.everydaycounselor.com. http://www.npmc.org/archives/sh/shistory.htm (accessed November 2006).
5. The original rings are kept in the Moravian archives at Herrnhut. The Greek wording is gender neutral and could equally be translated, "None of us lives for herself."
6. This quotation and those following are from the German original in the Moravian archives at Herrnhut, published by Johann Christoph Stöhr, Büdingen, 1740, translated by Markus Laegel, paraphrased into contemporary English, then checked against the original text for sense.
7. A. G. Spangenberg, *Leben Zinzendorfs* (1772-75), trans. L. T. Nyberg (1773), p. 75, footnote 1.
8. Zinzendorf's own life and liberty would be threatened on several occasions, and he would suffer the pain of losing close friends to both natural hazards and hostile persecution.
9. From "Rules of the Order of the Mustard Seed," Büdingen, 1740.

Chapter 3: The Return of the Knight

1. Some sources attribute this painting to Domenico Feti, others to Sternberg. The image can be viewed at http://zinzendorf.com/feti.htm.
2. John R. Weinlick, *Count Zinzendorf* (Bethlehem, PA: Moravian Church in America, 1956), p. 44, quoting A. G. Spangenberg, *Leben Zinzendorfs* (1772-75), trans. Samuel Jackson (1838), p. 20.

3. James E. Hutton, *A History of the Moravian Church* (London: Moravian Publication Office, 1909), sec. 2.1.
4. Biographical details on de Noailles are taken from "Louis-Antoine de Noailles," *The Catholic Encyclopaedia Online*. http://www.newadvent.org/cathen/11085b.htm (accessed November 2006).
5. Jansenism was a stream within the Catholic Church that emphasised personal piety and morality but had certain similarities to Calvinism in its understanding of salvation.
6. Weinlick, *Count Zinzendorf*, p. 57 (quoting Spangenberg, *Leben Zinzendorfs*).
7. Spangenberg, *Leben Zinzendorfs*, p. 37.
8. Hutton, *A History of the Moravian Church*, sec. 2.1.
9. Christian David's testimony, along with others from Herrnhut, is recorded in *The Journal of John Wesley* from August 1738.
10. Weinlick, *Count Zinzendorf*, p. 37.
11. Hutton, *A History of the Moravian Church*, sec. 2.3.
12. Historical details from Paul Brickhill, *The Dam Busters* (London: Pan Books Ltd., 1954), n.p.

Chapter 4: The Hidden Seed

1. Episcopal succession is the practice of commissioning priests through laying on of hands by a bishop, in an unbroken line leading back to Christ's first apostles. The Brethren considered this practice to be valuable in identifying them with the historical Christian faith and sought out the Waldensians because no bishop of the state church would be willing to grant them official status in this way.
2. This assertion is a reasoned generalization. There is no reliable evidence of the Brethren Church ever declaring military or political allegiances. In the later years, there were clearly individual members with political involvement, but even then many chose to act out of conviction rather than self-interest in the circumstances they faced. See James E. Hutton, *A History of the Moravian Church* (London: Moravian Publication Office, 1909), pp. 1.3–15.
3. J. A. Comenius, *The Labyrinth of the World and the Paradise of the Heart* (1623), trans. Louthan/Sterk (Mahwah, NJ: Paulist Press, 1998), p. 27.
4. Hutton, *A History of the Moravian Church*, sec. 1.16.
5. J. McGee, "High Flight," from the original held in the U.S. Library of Congress, USAF History Support Office website.

Chapter 5: Summer of '27

1. Four of the twelve were then chosen by lot to be chief elders, and this role also fell to Christian David.
2. A. J. Lewis, *Zinzendorf the Ecumenical Pioneer* (London: SCM Press, 1962), p. 58. Translation updated into contemporary language.
3. A bite-sized pastry dish traditionally eaten at Christmas in the UK. The sweet filling (mincemeat) is sold in jars and is very tasty . . . once put in the pie and properly cooked!
4. The wild goose was used as a symbol for the Holy Spirit in the early Celtic Church.
5. Letter held in the Moravian archives, Herrnhut.

Chapter 6: Prayer Ignition

1. Eberhard Bethge, *Dietrich Bonhoeffer: Man of Vision—Man of Courage* (New York: Harper and Row, 1970).
2. A. J. Lewis, *Zinzendorf the Ecumenical Pioneer* (London: SCM Press, 1962), p. 179.
3. The group of 48 were the first to be identified by name. The initial volunteers were 14 young men, soon to be joined by 28 women(!), with numbers then rapidly growing to

around 70. Spangenberg also notes that "the [spiritually] awakened children . . . also arranged something of a similar kind amongst themselves." See A. G. Spangenberg, *Leben Zinzendorfs (1772–75)*, trans. Samuel Jackson (1838), p. 88.

4. Attributed to Spangenberg. He quotes the biblical basis and inspiration as Isaiah 62:6-7.
5. Spangenberg, *Leben Zinzendorfs*, p. 136.
6. For loads of inspiration and resources around continuous prayer, visit www.24-7prayer.com.
7. The terms "the Lamb of God" and "the Lamb who was slain" are used to describe Christ's sacrificial death on the cross and were the central themes of Zinzendorf's theology.
8. To see the impact that the Losung had on the start of 24-7, read Pete Greig and Dave Roberts, *Red Moon Rising* (US: Relevant, 2003; UK: Kingsway, 2004), chapter 13. To receive the texts by e-mail, visit www.moravian.org/daily_texts/.
9. John R. Weinlick, *Count Zinzendorf* (Bethlehem, PA: Moravian Church in America, 1956), p. 87.
10. A. G. Spangenberg, *An Exposition of Christian Doctrine, as Taught in the Protestant Church of the United Brethren, or Unitas Fratrum* (Bath, UK: S. Hazard Printer, 1796), p. 403.
11. Weinlick, *Count Zinzendorf*, p. 91.
12. The Journal of John Wesley, 8 August 1738.

Chapter 7: Then Slave I Shall Be
1. James E. Hutton, *A History of the Moravian Church* (London: Moravian Publication Office, 1909), sec. 2.6.
2. John R. Weinlick, *Count Zinzendorf* (Bethlehem, PA: Moravian Church in America, 1956), p. 84.
3. A. J. Lewis, *Zinzendorf the Ecumenical Pioneer* (London: SCM Press, 1962), p. 84.
4. Philip H. Smith, *General History of Duchess County 1609 to 1876* (Pawling, NY, 1877). Language slightly updated.
5. Weinlick, *Count Zinzendorf*, p. 145.
6. Hutton, *A History of the Moravian Church*, sec. 2.7.
7. "Genadendal: Valley of Grace," Museums Online South Africa. http://www.museums.org.za/genadendal (accessed November 2006).

Chapter 8: On the Road and Off the Rails
1. John R. Weinlick, *Count Zinzendorf* (Bethlehem, PA: Moravian Church in America, 1956), p. 111.
2. Taken from 1 Peter 1:1, referencing John 11:52.
3. A. J. Lewis, *Zinzendorf the Ecumenical Pioneer* (London: SCM Press, 1962), p. 120.
4. See Romans 2:14-15; 7:16,18,22.
5. Quoted in Karl Olsson, *By One Spirit* (Chicago, IL: Covenant Publications, 1962), p. 17.
6. James E. Hutton, *A History of the Moravian Church* (London: Moravian Publication Office, 1909), sec. 2.5.
7. Weinlick, *Count Zinzendorf*, p. 127.
8. Hutton, *A History of the Moravian Church*, sec. 2.14.
9. This phrase was first coined by the Lutheran theologian Rupert Meldenius, a contemporary of Comenius, who then brought it into use within the remnant of the Bohemian Brethren. It was also a favorite saying of the Pietist leader Philip Spener, which is how Zinzendorf first came to use it. See John R. Weinlick and Albert Frank, *The Moravian Church Through the Ages* (Bethlehem, PA: Moravian Church in America, 1996), p. 41.

10. A. G. Spangenberg, *Leben Zinzendorfs* (1772–75), trans. Samuel Jackson (1838), p. 317.
11. The idea is based on biblical verses such as 1 Corinthians 4:10: "We are fools for Christ."
12. The actual language used was, of course, mostly eighteenth-century German. These phrases convey something of the level and meaning in contemporary English.
13. Hutton, *A History of the Moravian Church*, sec. 2.8.

Chapter 9: 'Twas on the Good Ship *Simmonds*
1. *The Journal of John Wesley*, ed. P. L. Parker (Kent, UK: STL Productions). Wesley's version is corroborated by the journal of David Nitschmann, who also notes, "There was great fright among the people who have no God. . . . I was content, for our lives are in God's hands."
2. Ibid., February 7, 1736.
3. J. Byous, in correspondence.
4. Attributed to the journal of Johann Martin Bolzius, minister of the Salzburger Lutherans in Georgia.
5. The first provincial Grand Master of the Savannah lodge was Roger Lacy in 1735–1736, but the fact of Oglethorpe's involvement is generally acknowledged.
6. *The Journal of John Wesley*, February 14, 1736.
7. Letter reproduced in Wittig, *Texts of Mission*, trans. Markus Laegel.
8. *The Journal of John Wesley*, January 24, 1738.
9. Ibid., March 4, 1738.
10. James E. Hutton, *A History of the Moravian Church* (London: Moravian Publication Office, 1909), sec. 2.9.
11. *The Journal of John Wesley*, May 24, 1738.
12. Ibid., August 14, 1738.
13. Hutton, *A History of the Moravian Church*, sec. 2.9.
14. Molther advocated a doctrine of "stillness," or quietism, which held that any form of personal effort or initiative (including participation in the traditional sacraments of the Church) was irrelevant to the pursuit of salvation. This was at odds both with Wesley's own views and with the general Moravian tradition of practical spirituality.
15. Elie Halevy, *A History of the English People in 1815* (1913), trans. Watkins and Barker (New York: Harcourt Brace, 1924).
16. At this stage, the Methodists were officially still operating within the Anglican Church.

Chapter 10: To the Ends of the Earth
1. James E. Hutton, *A History of the Moravian Church* (London: Moravian Publication Office, 1909), sec. 2.6.
2. A. G. Spangenberg, *Leben Zinzendorfs* (1772–75), trans. Samuel Jackson (1838), p. 502.
3. Hutton, *A History of the Moravian Church*, sec. 2.14.
4. Ibid., sec. 2.6.
5. John 12:24-25 (*THE MESSAGE*, adapted. I have used "seed" instead of "grain of wheat.")

The Renewed Order of the Mustard Seed
1. Pete Greig, *The Vision and the Vow* (Lake Mary, FL: Relevant Books, 2004).
2. Matthew 22:36-40; 28:18-20.

BIBLIOGRAPHY

I have included reference details for my sources in the endnotes, but the following titles are ones that I drew on more heavily, and they deserve a mention in their own right.

Comenius, Jan Amos. *The Labyrinth of the World and the Paradise of the Heart* (1623), trans. Louthan/Sterk. Mahwah, NJ: Paulist Press, 1998.

> Although written a century earlier, Comenius's classic beautifully captures the ideals of the Bohemian Brethren, many of which were genuinely restored during the renewal under Zinzendorf. The book is in two parts: The "Labyrinth" is an incisive critique of the late medieval world at its darkest, but in many places feels eerily relevant to our own society, which in some respects has progressed little in 400 years; the "Paradise" offers a compelling alternative, a beautiful vision of the life that can and should be possible for disciples who submit all to the love and lordship of Christ.

Hutton, James E. *A History of the Moravian Church*. London: Moravian Publication Office, 1909.

> Hutton traces an exhaustive history of the Moravian church from its beginnings in Bohemia to the end of the nineteenth century. He provides a full history of the rise and fall of the Bohemian Brethren and is also especially strong on the early works in England and America. His perspective is unashamedly Moravian, as he is tracing the history of the current denomination. The book is available as a free e-text via Project Gutenberg, with a

slightly more readable HTML version that may be found at http://everydaycounselor.com/hutton.

Lewis, A. J. *Zinzendorf the Ecumenical Pioneer.* London: SCM Press, 1962.

Lewis's work is also written as a biography, but with a deliberate focus on Zinzendorf's pioneering ideas on church unity and mission.

Parker, P. L., ed. *The Journal of John Wesley.* Kent, UK: STL Productions.

John Wesley, the founder of the Methodist Church, kept copious journals from the start of his ill-fated mission to Georgia in 1735 to a few months before his death in 1791. They provide insight into the man himself and the everyday world in which he lived. Wesley gives a firsthand account of his conversations with the Moravian Peter Böhler, his "conversion" experience, and his visits to Herrnhut and Herrnhaag at the height of their early development (which Parker unfortunately leaves out of his single-volume edition).

Spangenberg, Augustus Gottlieb. *Leben Zinzendorfs* (1772–1775). Spangenberg was Zinzendorf's close friend and co-worker, who 12 years after Zinzendorf's death undertook to write the comprehensive story of Zinzendorf's life. The strength of his work is that it draws on eyewitness accounts and contemporary knowledge. The weakness is that he wrote without the benefit of hindsight and while still embroiled in the many public controversies surrounding Zinzendorf and the Moravian church. It is said that they drew lots to determine whether

Spangenberg should write an unbiased warts-and-all account or a more robust "defense" of Zinzendorf, and the lot fell in favor of the positive version "for the encouragement of the Brethren." Spangenberg's preface states clearly that he has made strenuous efforts to be truthful and unbiased in his writing, but he is clearly sympathetic in his choice of material. There are two English translations: Samuel Jackson's version (1838) is the easier read, but is slightly abridged; L. T. Nyberg (1773) translated the first two volumes in full, including the sometimes crucial footnotes, but authentic eighteenth-century English (including the use of the letter "f" for "s") makes it a tougher challenge!

Weinlick, John R. *Count Zinzendorf.* Bethlehem, PA: Moravian Church in America, 1956.

Weinlick is probably the standard English-language biography of Zinzendorf, and it provides a good intro-duction for anyone wanting to read a straight historical account of his life and work.

Weinlick, John R., and Albert Frank. *The Moravian Church Through the Ages.* Bethlehem, PA: Moravian Church in America, 1996.

Although much shorter than Hutton, Weinlick and Frank provide a concise and readable summary of the Moravian church, from the influence of Wycliffe and Hus through the renewal under Zinzendorf and into the late twentieth century.

About the Author

Phil Anderson is a pilot and pilgrim, an engineer and encourager, a communicator and conspirator. He works as a consultant, serves as a leader of Thurrock Christian Fellowship in southeast England, participates as a member of 24-7 Prayer (an international community of prayer, mission and justice) and facilitates www.mustardseedorder.com, an online meeting place for those interested in exploring the relevance of Zinzendorf's Mustard Seed vow to discipleship in the twenty-first century. He is a husband to Lisa and a father to Holly (9) and Bethany (7).

ADDITIONAL RESOURCES FROM

24-7

*Red Moon Rising: The Adventure of Faith
and the Power of Prayer*
by Pete Greig and Dave Roberts
The amazing story of the birth of the
24-7 Prayer movement
(Relevant/USA, 2003; Survivor/UK, 2004;
Brockhaus/Germany, 2005;
Päivä/Finland, 2005; Torch Trust for the Blind
[audio]/UK, 2006)

*The Vision and the Vow: Rules of Life
and Rhythms of Grace*
by Pete Greig
A contemporary call to discipleship exploring the
words of Pete Greig's poem "The Vision," which
has touched more than one million people
(Survivor/UK, 2004; Relevant/USA, 2004)

*The 24-7 Prayer Manual: A Guide to Creating and
Sustaining Holy Space in the Real World*
Everything you need to know to set up and
run a night-and-day prayer room
(Survivor/UK, 2003; Cook
Communications/USA, 2005)

God on Mute: Engaging the Silence of
Unanswered Prayer
A look at some of the hard questions about
unanswered prayer and suffering
(Survivor/UK, 2007; Regal Books/USA, 2007)

PunkMonk
by Andy Freeman and Pete Greig
(Regal/USA, 2007; Survivor/UK, 2007)

[24-7 TITLES]
WWW.24-7PRAYER.COM

Writing at its best is a conversation, not a lecture. The Internet has added new dimensions and possibilities to this conversation. I would love to hear your own thoughts, insights, reactions and stories in response to this account. You can e-mail me directly at contact@ philanderson.org (I can't guarantee a personal reply, but I will read everything that is sent to me). Alternatively, for loads of stuff I couldn't fit in the book, including links, feedback and comments, visit www.philanderson.org/lotr.

Engaging the Silence of Unanswered Prayer

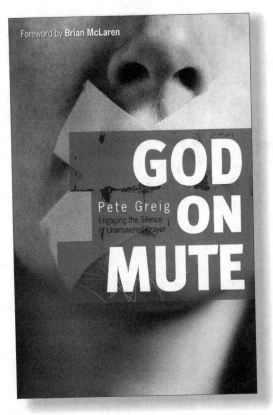

Foreword by **Brian McLaren**

Pete Greig
Engaging the Silence
of Unanswered Prayer

GOD ON MUTE

God on Mute
978.08307.43247

Pete Greig, the acclaimed author of *Red Moon Rising*, has written his most intensely personal and honest book yet in *God on Mute*, a work born out of his wife Samie's fight for her life. Greig asks the timeless questions of what it means to suffer and to pray and to suffer through the silence because your prayers seem unanswered. This silence, Greig relates, is the hardest thing. The world collapses. Then all goes quiet. Words can't explain, don't fit, won't work. People avoid you and don't know what to say. So you turn to Him and you pray. You need Him more than ever before. But some-how…even God Himself seems on mute. In this heart-searching, honest and deeply profound book, Pete Greig looks at the hard side of prayer, how to respond when there seem to be no answers and how to cope with those who seek to interpret our experience for us. Here is a story of faith, hope and love beyond all understanding.